Pastoral Counseling and Preaching

Books by Donald Capps
Published by The Westminster Press

*Pastoral Counseling and Preaching:
A Quest for an Integrated Ministry*

Pastoral Care: A Thematic Approach

Pastoral Counseling and Preaching: A Quest for an Integrated Ministry

Donald Capps

The Westminster Press
Philadelphia

First edition

Published by The Westminster Press ®
Philadelphia, Pennsylvania

PRINTED IN THE UNITED STATES OF AMERICA
9 8 7 6 5 4 3 2 1

Acknowledgment for use of excerpts from copyrighted materials:

Abingdon Press, from *Casebook in Pastoral Counseling,* by Newman S. Cryer and John Monroe Vayhinger. Copyright © 1962 by Abingdon Press.

Houghton Mifflin Company and Constable and Company, from *On Becoming a Person,* by Carl R. Rogers. Copyright © 1961 by Carl R. Rogers.

Human Sciences Press, from "Biblical Models of Pastoral Counseling," by Donald Capps, *Pastoral Psychology,* Vol. 28. Copyright © 1979 by Human Sciences Press.

The Society for Promoting Christian Knowledge and William B. Eerdmans Publishing Co., Inc., from *The End of Man,* by Austin Farrer. Copyright 1973 by The Society for Promoting Christian Knowledge.

The University of Chicago Press and Albert L. Blackwell, from "Schleiermacher's Sermon at Nathanael's Grave," by Albert L. Blackwell, *Journal of Religion,* Vol. 57. Copyright © 1977 by The University of Chicago. All rights reserved.

Library of Congress Cataloging in Publication Data

Capps, Donald.
    Pastoral counseling and preaching.

    Includes bibliographical references.
    1. Pastoral counseling. 2. Preaching. I. Title.
BV4012.2.C27   253   80–18502
ISBN 0–664–24342–8

To Florence and Leonard

Contents

Preface

What is the relationship between pastoral counseling and preaching? Does one's counseling influence one's preaching? Does one's preaching influence one's counseling? Do these two functions of ministry go together or not?

In the 1950's and early 1960's, pastors could not easily ignore these questions. They agreed that these questions have important professional, theological, methodological, and cultural implications.

Professionally, these questions challenged the assumption that the primary role of the Protestant minister is to preach. The emergence of pastoral counseling as an important function of ministry caused many ministers to decide that counseling would play the major role in shaping their ministry. This shift from preaching to a ministry based on counseling was largely due to the inherent attractiveness of counseling. But it was also due to ministers' doubts about the effectiveness of preaching. Through pastoral counseling, one could become involved in the real problems of people instead of speaking in vague generalities from the safety of the pulpit.

Theologically, these questions challenged traditional views about the communication of the gospel. Proponents of preaching cited the virtues of proclamation. For the gospel to be heard and acted on, it must first be proclaimed. What better vehicle than the Sunday morning sermon? But proponents of pastoral counseling doubted that communication of the gospel is mainly verbal proclamation. They considered the communication of the gospel an act of kenosis, of assuming the burden of another person's problems and abandoning oneself in the act of "being with" vulnerable, suffering, and distressed persons. Thus, the gospel is communicated by the pastor's human presence.

These questions also concerned methods of ministry. Edgar Jackson pointed out in 1961 that the average pastor has difficulty synthesizing the functions of preaching and counseling: "How is he to adjust the more directive mood of the pulpit with the more non-directive mood of the counseling room? Where does he as an individual find his true relationship to this dual function without destroying the integrity of his own growing personality?"[1] The issue here is not only that preaching is more verbal than counseling, or even that preaching is one-way communication while counseling is dialogical. It is rather that they use different methods. In preaching, the minister is directive. In counseling, the approach is nondirective. When Jackson wrote these words in 1961, the dominant method in pastoral counseling was client-centered. This tended to dramatize the difference between preaching and counseling methods.

These questions also meant exploring the relationship between Christianity and modern culture. For many proponents of pastoral counseling, preaching-centered ministry tends to insulate ministry from its cultural context. Preaching can rely wholly on Scripture and doctrine, while a counseling ministry must open itself to psychological theories and methods. Thus, counseling-centered ministry means openness to contemporary culture through its psychological disciplines. Proponents of pastoral counseling viewed Paul Tillich's work as a theological justification for their point of view, and branded the opposing perspective as "too Barthian" in its exclusive emphasis on proclamation of the Word.

In short, these questions concerning the relationship between preaching and counseling posed fundamental professional, theological, methodological, and cultural issues.

These issues are no less urgent today. But exploring the relationship between preaching and pastoral counseling is no longer considered a means of addressing them.

This book deals with the relationship between preaching and pastoral counseling. My thesis is that both can reflect common understandings of the theory and practice of ministry, that their differences on professional, theological, methodological, and cultural grounds can be bridged. Preaching and pastoral counseling need not be antithetical to each other; they can be two foci of an integrated ministry. Not only can preaching profit from pastoral counseling, but pastoral counseling also has much to gain from preaching. It is rarely proposed that pastoral counseling can benefit from preaching, even by those who advocate the integration of these two forms of ministry. Emphasis is almost always placed on the contribution that pastoral counseling skills can make toward effective preaching. True integration means mutual enrichment in theory and practice.

I want to thank the students at The Graduate Seminary of Phillips University for encouraging this project. I am also mindful that the memory of my boyhood pastor, Frank H. Hanson, has influenced this book in ways that I cannot fully fathom.

D.C.

Chapter 1

The Relationship of Preaching and Counseling

What grounds are there for relating preaching and pastoral counseling? How can we investigate this relationship? A good starting point is the existing literature on this topic. Much of the literature dates back to the period when this was a lively issue. This relationship between preaching and pastoral counseling has been viewed in three ways. First, some authors say that preaching is itself an act of pastoral counseling. When preachers enter the pulpit, they become counselors. They may proclaim the gospel, exhort parishioners to lead more godly lives, instruct them in the fundamentals of the Christian faith, and speak out against social injustice. But their main purpose is to give parishioners wise counsel for dealing with life's problems.

Second, some writers take the view that preaching and pastoral counseling have a common theological base. While preaching and pastoral counseling differ in style and mode of communication, their objectives reflect a common theological understanding of our relationship to God. Those who take this view contend that theological viewpoints made *explicit* in preaching are *implicit* in counseling theories and methods.

Third, some authors show how insights from psychological theories and methods clarify the communication process in preaching. Here the relation between preaching and pastoral counseling is mediated by psychology, particularly clinical and developmental theories that are as applicable to preaching as to pastoral counseling.

Preaching as Pastoral Counseling

Those who view preaching as counseling are not just saying that preaching opens the way for subsequent counseling sessions. Nor are they saying that preaching involves wise counsel *along with* proclamation, exhortation, instruction, and prophetic witness. They are saying that preaching is fundamentally an act of pastoral counseling.

Harry Emerson Fosdick developed the view that preaching is an act of pastoral counseling. According to Edmund Linn, Fosdick saw serious deficiencies in both expository and topical sermons, and sought to develop a more effective method called the "project method" of preaching, or the "counseling sermon."[2] Fosdick saw that sermons based on the exposition of a Biblical text give "an unwarranted importance to some passage in the Bible instead of to the business of living. . . . The congregation had come to church to become renewed in the resources of Christian living amid the problems then confronting them, not to hear a lengthy analysis of the life and times of Abraham, Moses, and John." Fosdick also believed that the topical sermon, while more relevant than the expository, has a serious weakness. It requires the minister "to be an authority in every field of human knowledge. The opinions of a preacher whose information is necessarily limited are little respected."

Fosdick intended the counseling sermon to avoid both pitfalls. Unlike the expository sermon, the counseling sermon begins with people's real problems. As he puts it, "We need more sermons that try to face people's real problems with them, meet their difficulties, answer their questions, confirm their noblest faiths and interpret their experiences in sympathetic, wise and understanding cooperation." Unlike the topical sermon, the counseling sermon does not require the preacher to be an expert on the major social and political issues of the day, but instead requires sensitivity to the way that modern life creates a multitude of personal problems for parishioners. The minister may not have detailed knowledge about a social problem and may not know how it could be solved. But one can know how problems of this nature impinge on parishioners' lives. This knowledge comes from familiarity with parishioners' daily struggles.

Linn lists the following characteristics of the counseling sermon:

1. *The counseling sermon expresses clear convictions based on personal experience.* The pastor needs to acquire and maintain a clear position on the problem preached about. Such conviction is acquired through personal experience and direct observations: "His own life, the behavior of his immediate family, observation of the contemporary scene, the knowledge of human nature gained by personal counseling, and witnessing the power of God at work in the transformation of individuals all contribute to giving form to the preacher's convictions."

2. *The counseling sermon involves speaking as to a single person.* The value of personal counseling lies in its attention to specific problems. Counseling sermons also need to focus on specific problems. This might mean that some parishioners' needs will be overlooked week after week, but the perceptive pastor will not fail to address these needs at the first opportunity. Moreover, preachers are more likely to address the needs of the many if they speak as to a single person than if they try to cover all these needs in every sermon. The latter approach results in mere generalities about many complex problems.

3. *The counseling sermon involves relating to people where they are.* Counseling preaching presupposes a deep understanding of the individuals within the congregation and of the complications of the world in which they live. With this approach, the minister must be in touch with the people to

discover their needs. Effective preaching depends on the minister's capacity to know where people are and to speak to that situation.

4. *The counseling sermon deals fairly with objections.* The preacher needs to anticipate listeners' objections. One wants to avoid any indication that these convictions are simplistic, that they fail to take adequate account of the complexity of the problem. Thus, in the course of the sermon, one needs to deal with objections fairly and dispassionately. As Linn puts it, "No matter how the unforeseen difficulties in the minds of the people are treated, the preacher should exert to the full his wisdom, understanding, and sympathy, never becoming arbitrary or dogmatic, but always seeking to be fair. Preaching is like having two people in the pulpit at once—the preacher and the antagonist—and the latter will have genuine doubts, questions, and yearnings."

5. *The counseling sermon applies the gospel to persons.* The counseling sermon does not involve exposition of Biblical passages, but this does not mean that the gospel of Jesus Christ is neglected. Through personal experience and observation, the pastor has witnessed the power of God in the transformation of individual lives, and therefore knows the truth of the gospel. The counseling sermon is based on the underlying conviction that "no person is ever beyond the reach of the correcting, healing, and consoling power of this gospel." Thus, the counseling sermon is not just a matter of commiserating with troubled people. It involves proclaiming the power and saving grace of the gospel of Jesus Christ. In this way, proclamation and counseling support each other.

6. *The counseling sermon retains the values of older methods.* The counseling sermon is not expository, but the Bible is indispensable in preaching because it sheds light on virtually every problem of modern living. The counseling sermon is not topical, but the best elements of the topical method can be used to show how personal problems have their origins in the complex social conditions of the modern world.

7. *The counseling sermon makes a directed effort.* Counseling preaching requires considerable effort to learn people's strengths and weaknesses. The sermon can be effective only if one has made a concerted effort to know the questions for which people seek answers. The preacher who fails to take the initiative to discover these concerns will not be effective in the pulpit. A sermon that is counseling in form but fails to speak to real needs is no better than an expository sermon on the life of Abraham, Moses, or John. In fact it may be worse, because it promises insight into personal problems and needs, but fails to make good on its promises.

These seven characteristics of the counseling sermon indicate how preaching can be understood as an act of pastoral counseling. How good is this approach? Certainly, it is better than the other approaches in the ways that Linn indicates. But we can raise several objections to its handling of the basic relationship of preaching and pastoral counseling. From the preaching perspective, one can question the view that counseling is preeminent over proclamation, exhortation, teaching, prophetic witness, and other important aspects of preaching. The expository and topical methods have their weaknesses, but this does not mean that proclamation, exhortation, teaching, and prophetic witness ought therefore to be subordinated to counseling. If we say that counseling is the function of preaching to which all others are subordinate, are we not committing the same fallacy as preaching theories that define it as proclamation? Moreover, the claim that preaching is fundamentally proclamation has a certain face validity that this claim lacks.

A second objection to this approach is that no real attempt is made to clarify how counseling is being understood. Since Fosdick's method was developed in the 1930's, it would be unfair to expect it to be informed by a well-defined counseling theory. Pastoral counseling itself was not informed by good counseling theories. In fact, some argue that Fosdick's preaching method influenced the development of pastoral counseling. Paul C. Vitz[3] notes that the title of one of Carl Rogers' major books, *On Becoming a Person,* is remarkably similar to Fosdick's classic, *On Becoming a Real Person.* Vitz goes beyond this surface similarity and notes that Fosdick, like Rogers, emphasized the importance of self-discovery and self-acceptance, and gave special attention to the discrepancy between a person's ideal self and his perceived or actual self. Thus, there is a nascent counseling theory in Fosdick's preaching method that, if explicated, might have had striking similarities to Rogers' client-centered therapy.

As it stands, however, Fosdick's counseling sermon approach is not clear about what it understands counseling to be. What kind of counseling does Fosdick have in mind? Directive or nondirective? Does it emphasize insight or behavioral change? Fosdick's preaching method does not address these questions. As a result, its understanding of counseling remains extremely vague. A method of preaching that is oriented to counseling can no longer avoid these fundamental questions.

David K. Switzer has recently addressed these questions in *Pastor, Preacher, Person.*[4] He points to Robert H. Carkhuff's conclusion in *Helping and Human Relations* that "all effective interpersonal processes share a common core of conditions conducive to facilitative human experiences," with such conditions normally provided by the helping professional. These conditions include accurate empathy, respect, concreteness, genuineness, self-disclosure, confrontation, and immediacy. Switzer than shows how the preacher can employ these elements of effective interpersonal processes in the pulpit. For example, confrontation in counseling is neither accusatory nor punitive, but involves perceiving discrepancies in the counselee's words or actions and raising questions about them. Using similar methods of confrontation in preaching, the pastor creates conditions conducive to the changes typically sought in "prophetic" preaching.

This example illustrates how counseling principles can be applied to preaching. As Switzer puts it, "These seven ingredients in great amounts and quality must be a part of all relationships which we have with other persons if we want those relationships to be helpful and growth-producing for them as well as fulfilling for ourselves. This has been quite adequately substantiated by psychotherapeutic research and clinical practice. Since preaching, however we may talk about it theologically, is clearly an interpersonal process to which the adjective 'helping' can hopefully be applied, the assumption is made that the conditions necessary to elicit deeper self-exploration, increase of insight, motivation to change, evaluation of behavioral alternatives, the facilitation of the decision-making process, and the acting on the basis of those decisions, would be the same, although somewhat differently expressed because of the unique nature of the preacher-congregation relationship. Therefore, the conscious introduction of these conditions into the preaching process would seem to be a necessary precondition for the effective proclamation of the Word of God." Switzer's discussion of these seven conditions and their use in preaching could provide the "preaching as pastoral counseling" approach the counseling theory it needs. In fact, his discussion is thoroughly consistent with the basic characteristics of Fosdick's approach to preaching.

The Common Theological Basis of Preaching and Pastoral Counseling

A second approach to the relationship of preaching and pastoral counseling explores their common theological foundations. Authors who take this approach want to show that preaching and counseling have similar theological bases and therefore contribute to an integrated ministry.

Thomas C. Oden is a good representative of this viewpoint. In his book *Kerygma and Counseling,* [5] Oden says that pastoral counseling needs to be informed by a theology of proclamation. Because preaching is primarily an act of proclamation, the idea that pastoral counseling is also informed by a theology of proclamation provides them a common theological foundation.

In developing this view, Oden points out that the good news of the Christian proclamation ("God is with us and for us") is the *explicit* basis of preaching and the *implicit* basis of counseling. Through preaching, listeners are explicitly told that "You are elected by God's love whether or not you receive and affirm your election. You are the son of the Father no matter to what extent you take your inheritance and flee to a far country." In counseling, the pastor communicates the same message, but in a nonverbal way:

> When the pastor performs his function as a counselor, his faith is becoming active in love. Here proclamation and therapy support one another in a total ministry of witness and mission. The love of God to which he witnesses in preaching is recapitulated in an analogous fashion in the empathy of counseling.

In counseling, the relationship between counselor and counselee communicates the love of God. In preaching, this same love of God is announced in a clear, decisive proclamation. Thus, pastoral counseling and preaching communicate the same reality, but preaching does it through the spoken word, while counseling does it through the relationship of counselor to counselee.

This raises some questions about the inherent limitations of pastoral counseling. As Oden puts it: "If kerygmatic proclamation is so indispensable for the clarification of the reality of acceptance, why should it not be imperative for the effective therapist then to become a preacher? For how can there by any genuinely deep self-acceptance as long as the client is unaware of the word of divine acceptance?" The issue is whether divine acceptance must always be mediated verbally, or whether it can be mediated through an interpersonal relationship. Oden contends that "liberating divine acceptance can be mediated concretely through interpersonal relationships without overt witness to its ground and source." He concludes that the counselor's task is to communicate an accepting reality through the relationship itself. True, there may be special times when the counselor makes verbal reference to the source of this accepting reality. However, "the moment he does, he ceases being a counselor and becomes a preacher." Moreover, when the counselor temporarily adopts this preaching role, it can prove difficult to shift back into the accepting relationship.

Thus, the relation between preaching and pastoral counseling is based on the good news of the gospel, especially its proclamation of God's love and acceptance. Oden emphasizes the reciprocal relationship of preaching and pastoral counseling, noting that

> counseling enriches preaching, since participating in the anguish, conflict, and perplexity of the parishioner enables the minister better to understand the depths of the human predicament. Furthermore, it is clear that since the Christian proclamation strengthens self-understanding, it also strengthens counseling.

But while they enrich each other, counseling and preaching are distinct functions of ministry. Counseling rarely involves direct proclamation of God's love and acceptance; it relies on the relationship to communicate the reality of God's love.

The strong point of Oden's approach is that he relates the two functions of ministry theologically. He does not relate them in terms of superficial similarities (e.g., style and technique), but bases their commonality on the divine-human relationship. There is no more fundamental theological issue than the relationship of God to man, and therefore pastoral counseling, like preaching, must deal with it. In this view, Oden has the support of Wayne E. Oates, who says that "the awareness of God *as* reality makes counseling pastoral."[6]

However, we can raise some important objections to Oden's distinction between preaching as explicit and pastoral counseling as implicit communication of this reality. It sets up an artificial distinction between the two that can be criticized from the perspectives of both.

From the counseling standpoint, Oden is right to warn against the use of strong proclamatory language. Certain kinds of verbalization common to preaching are inappropriate in counseling. There is much merit in Oden's criticism of the views of Thurneysen, Thilo, and other Swiss and German pastoral theologians who take the view that pastoral counseling must include overt proclamation of the gospel. While there are times when such proclamation is appropriate, it is usually best to avoid it because

> our temptation is very much more to become moralizers, judgers, and answer givers, introjecting our viewpoint and imposing it upon troubled persons, often ineffectually, rather than allowing them the freedom to discover the covenant at the center of their own personal existence through dwelling in the presence of a person who mediates the reality of God's acceptance relationally rather than verbally.

We can ask, however, whether Oden is being too rigid here. For him, proclamation always seems to imply verbal communication that is clear and decisive. But proclamation can also involve the cautious probing and the verbal subtlety found, for example, in the parables of Jesus. It can be subtle, not coercive, in its intrusiveness. If it can shout in mother's ear, it can also tug at mother's elbow.

Oden places unnecessarily severe restrictions on the communication of the gospel in pastoral counseling. When the gospel is considered the forceful proclamation of God's love, counseling is not a good setting for communicating it. This need not be the case, however, when proclamation is more nuanced, though no less incisive.

A second basis for opening pastoral counseling to verbal proclamation of the gospel is Oden's own statement that proclamation involves communicating "the relation of Christ to human brokenness." If this is so, one important aspect of proclamation is to assess this human brokenness. This aspect of proclamation has been critically important to preaching, because the affirmation of God's love is intended to heal this brokenness. In a similar way, counseling could also involve assessment of human brokenness as experienced by the counselee. If so, this would be an instance in which proclamation could take an explicitly verbal form.

Oden does not consider this possibility. He wants to emphasize how the counselor *embodies* Christ's relationship to human brokenness and, in so doing, relates to the counselee's sense of brokenness at a deeper level than words:

> Just as the incarnation witnesses to the God who does not just diagnose or analyze man's needs but actively participates in them, likewise effective counseling is not just objective diagnosis of the individual's conflict but active empathetic involvement in the patient's suffering.

While the incarnational dimension of the relationship between counselor and counselee is extremely important, especially in its concern with human brokenness, its verbal counterpart need not be limited to "objective diagnosis of the individual's conflict." Such assessment or diagnosis can also be based on proclamation. This would not be an "objective" assessment of the counselee's situation, but a theological assessment of the counselee's brokenness and need for divine love and acceptance.

Paul W. Pruyser makes a proposal along these lines when he recommends the use of theological themes as diagnostic variables.[7] Such themes as awareness of the holy, providence, faith, vocation, communion, repentance, and grace can provide guideposts for diagnosing the counselee's situation. The absence of any of these themes would indicate the nature and degree of brokenness in this person. Pruyser warns against indiscriminate use of theological language in communicating this diagnosis to the counselee, but he does not say that such words as faith, vocation, repentance, or grace should be avoided.

Pruyser's is not the only proposal for introducing theological language into the counseling process. John B. Cobb, Jr., in *Theology and Pastoral Care,* says that the best preaching

of modern times has reflected the creative tension between
Biblical language and the language of the contemporary
world, but pastoral counseling has relinquished the use of
Biblical language because it is likely to be counterproductive.
He contends that "the time may have come for us to bring
our language-world and that of the Bible together, while
allowing the biblical language to retain its own meaning."
Should this happen, "pastoral counselors could experience
their counseling not simply as in continuity with Christianity
in its ultimate purposes but as informed by the Christian
heritage in both form and substance." Like Pruyser, Cobb
worries about the indiscriminate use of Biblical language in
pastoral counseling. If used, "it must grow out of the living
experience of Christian people who are fully immersed in the
modern world. They must find that the authentic use of
biblical language illumines their experience and brings to
consciousness aspects of that experience that have been neglected or obscured by modern conceptualities. It must become natural to think partly in biblical language, not only in
hothouses of piety or in the interpretation of very special
experiences, but in the understanding of ordinary life. If this
occurs, and only when it occurs, will it become proper and
natural to employ such language in pastoral counseling."[8]

Admittedly, the idea that pastoral counseling may involve
verbal proclamation of a special kind is a sensitive issue with
pastoral counselors. Some pastoral counselors have ruled out
the use of "theological jargon" entirely, while others have
allowed for its use in special circumstances.[9] Few make a
strong case for its use in pastoral counseling. Nonetheless, by
limiting proclamation (both in its assessment of the human
condition and its affirmation of divine love and acceptance)
to the *relationship* between counselor and counselee, we impose an artificial restriction on the pastoral counselor. Oden
is certainly correct in saying that the "liberating Word can
be effectually embodied in relationships in which language is
not even necessary." But why is theological language the only
verbal expression that is explicitly and self-consciously ex-

cluded from the pastoral counseling setting?

Objections to Oden can also be raised from the perspective of preaching. If he places undue restrictions on verbal proclamation in pastoral counseling, he also says less than might be said for the *relationship* between preacher and listeners in the proclamation of the gospel. Does preaching manifest the same relationship that occurs in pastoral counseling? Does it also embody the pain of human brokenness and the affirmation of God's love and acceptance? Oden does not say whether preaching simply lacks this relationship, or whether preaching includes both the relationship and the verbal communication of the divine reality that it represents. The question of whether counseling might inform preaching through its insights into the nature of effective relationships is not seriously addressed.

Henri Nouwen takes up this issue in *Creative Ministry.* [10] This book is vitally concerned with the integration of various functions of ministry. From this concern, Nouwen says that preaching needs to reflect the insights the pastor gains from involvement in the lives of parishioners. Such insights are gained from the whole range of pastoral activities, not just counseling. But Nouwen's identification of two major features of the relation between preacher and listener is strongly influenced by the counseling relationship.

This relationship involves a *capacity for dialogue* and *availability.* By capacity for dialogue, Nouwen means "a way of relating to men and women so that they are able to respond to what is said with their own life experience." Through words, preachers effect a dialogue between their own life experiences and those of listeners. The listeners respond to these words because they find anchor places in their own life experiences. The listener wants to say, "Yes, I find myself in your words because your words come from the depths of human experiences and, therefore, are not just yours but also mine, and your insights do not just belong to you, but are mine as well." Capacity for dialogue of this sort requires the preacher to enter into a relationship in which partners can really influence each other. In a true dialogue the preacher cannot stay on the outside. He cannot remain untouchable and invulnerable. He has to be totally and most personally involved. This can be a completely internal process in which there is no verbal exchange of words, but it requires the risk of real engagement in the relationship between he who speaks and those who listen. Only then can we talk about a real dialogue.

This dialogue is similar to what happens in counseling, especially counseling that places a high premium on insight. Nouwen characterizes the respective roles of preacher and listener in this way: "But whenever the anxious and impenetrable man is approached by a fellow man who expresses his solidarity with him and offers his insight and understanding as a source of recognition and clarification, then his confusion can be taken away and paths that may lead to light can become visible." These roles are similar to those of the counselor and counselee. The counselor expresses solidarity with the counselee and offers insight so that the counselee can see new possibilities in life.

By availability Nouwen means that the preacher puts "the full-range of his life-experiences—his experiences in prayer, in conversation and in his lonely hours—at the disposal of those who ask him to be their preacher." In doing this, the preacher enables listeners to face their own condition and open themselves to life experiences they have previously avoided. Nouwen acknowledges that it is not easy for preachers to make the full range of their experience available to their listeners, because to be available to others requires being available to oneself. This means overcoming the tendency to look at only those dimensions of one's life experience that are consistent with the public image one seeks to project. On the other hand, Nouwen emphasizes that communicating one's availability to personal life experience does not mean reporting one's life experiences from the pulpit. The use of such autobiographical references in sermons has nothing to do with availability. Personal life experiences are not the *subject* but the *source* of communication. When they are the source, the sermon can then articulate with the life experiences of the listener. Nouwen quotes Carl Rogers' comment in this regard: "What is most personal is most general." He then cites Oden's commentary on Rogers' statement:

> Repeatedly I have found, to my astonishment, that the feelings which have seemed to me most private, most personal, and therefore the feelings I least expect to be understood by others, when clearly expressed, resonate deeply and consistently with their own experience. This has led me to believe that what I experience in the most unique and personal way, if brought to clear expression, is precisely what others are most deeply experiencing in analogous ways.[11]

In short, Nouwen's discussion of the preacher's capacity for dialogue and availability indicates that preaching can involve the same kind of interpersonal relationship as counseling.

In evaluating Oden's approach to the relationship of preaching and pastoral counseling, I have applauded his emphasis on their common theological foundations but criticized his distinctions between their methods of communication and their forms of relationship. These distinctions can be attributed to the tendency of pastoral theologians in the 1960's to differentiate *directive* and *nondirective* functions of ministry. When this distinction is applied to pastoral functions, preaching is typically judged the most directive and counseling the least directive. Oden's distinction between verbal communication and relationship is informed by this directive vs. nondirective polarity.

Psychology of Preaching Methods

A third approach to the relation between preaching and pastoral counseling is the use of psychological theories to assess preaching methods. This approach suggests that psychology, particularly clinical and developmental theories, can be used to evaluate various preaching methods. The use of psychological theories to assess preaching methods is not new. In 1918 Charles S. Gardner used the functional psychologies then current to assess the effects of different preaching methods on modern audiences.[12]

I would like to discuss two more recent examples of this approach. The first is the use of group dynamics theory to explore the effect of different preaching methods on listeners. The second involves the use of developmental theory to clarify the influence of preachers' attitudes on their preaching methods.

Preaching method and group dynamics. An example of the first is Edgar N. Jackson's *A Psychology for Preaching.*[13] While claiming that this study was influenced by Fosdick and the counseling sermon method, Jackson does not focus on counseling as such, but instead uses group dynamics theory to evaluate a congregation's response to different preaching methods. Through an experiment in which two different theories of group therapy were applied in preaching, Jackson shows that one type of sermon communicates to the group as a whole while another type communicates to isolated individuals within the larger group.

This experiment involved the use of two preaching methods based on different group therapy models. The first type was based on the "repressive-inspirational" method of group therapy. This method, employed by Alcoholics Anonymous with considerable success, represses the unpleasant and irritating features of life and emphasizes the inspirational. Jackson says that the

> repressive-inspirational method is particularly effective with an obsessive-compulsive type of personality which needs to be continually shored up or buttressed in order to face the onslaught of what it considers to be an unpleasant reality. The inner resources to sustain life are so weak that they must be supplemented by a regular ration of external support.

The second type was based on the "analytic" method of group therapy. This method tries "to discover the inner resources that are available to deal with [life] realistically and competently. . . . It believes in the innate capacity of each individual to deal with life's problems without escape and with candor." This method was used in the small groups that John Wesley organized for self-examination and spiritual growth.

In the experiment, sermons based on these two group therapy models were preached on alternate Sundays to the same congregation over a sixteen-week period. Trained observers recorded the reactions of the congregation to each type of sermon. Jackson found that when the repressive-inspirational sermon was being preached,

> there was a comfortable, relaxed feeling evident in the congregation. There was a ready and willing response. The members of the group seemed to be participating as a group who were bound together in a mood of pleasure and confidence, and there was little or no coughing.

In addition, members praised the sermon and remained after the service for informal conversation.

The analytic sermon evoked a wholly different response. The congregation was no less attentive, but it

> seemed to be broken up into individuals as questions were asked that had to be dealt with on individual terms. The feeling of identity as a group was at least partially lost. The sense of joy and responsiveness was replaced by a mood of introspection and uncomfortable self-examination. This was verified by the preacher who felt less response and almost a mood of antagonism as if the listeners had come for one thing and were given something else.

This attitude continued after the service. Parishioners spoke little to the minister as they left the church and did not gather on the lawn outside the church for friendly chats. As Jackson puts it, "people felt more concerned about themselves as persons than as parts of a sharing group." But Jackson also found that the analytic sermon was more likely to prompt individuals to request pastoral counseling. During the eight weeks that followed the analytic type of sermon, over two hundred hours of pastoral counseling were begun, with the largest single response after a sermon on jealousy. Thus, the repressive-inspirational sermon led to a greater sense of group solidarity, but the analytic sermon caused individuals to take more stock of their personal lives.

This experiment illustrates how group dynamics theory can identify the differential effects of preaching methods. It also had the unintended effect of shedding light on the relation between preaching and pastoral counseling. In discussing the potential effects of the counseling sermon, Edmund Linn had argued that "when a preacher speaks to the real condition of his people he soon discovers that he is being sought more and more by individuals who need to discuss their private personal problems. . . . One of the ultimate tests of the worth of a sermon is how many individuals want to see the minister alone."[14] Jackson's study indicates that people are likely to seek counseling if the sermon challenges individuals to submit to self-examination and self-criticism. The analytic sermon achieves greater success in speaking "as to a single person." The price of the success is a reduction in group solidarity.

Preaching method and developmental theory. A second example of the use of psychological theory to assess preaching methods is James E. Dittes' *Minister on the Spot.*[15] His main interest is the effect of ministers' attitudes on their preaching methods. His study is influenced by Erik H. Erikson's developmental theory, especially the first two stages of trust vs. mistrust, and autonomy vs. shame and self-doubt.

Dittes suggests that autonomy poses one of the most basic attitudinal dilemmas in one's preaching ministry. The minister wants to engage in preaching in an autonomous manner. How can he "let himself go to the preaching without becoming so enslaved to it that he cannot let it go when need be? This is freedom of investment."

But this freedom of investment is contradicted in two ways. One is *overinvestment* in preaching. For some, preaching is important not as *an* expression but as *the* expression of ministry. One not only masters techniques of Biblical exegesis and the art of communication but relies on these as evidence of faithfulness to one's vocation. The preaching role is not only the center of ministry. It is the form in which every function of ministry is carried out: "So that when one seeks him for personal counsel, is visited in the hospital, sits with him in a committee meeting or beside him at worship, one still must be made aware in tone and theme that here is the preacher." Such ministers are not free to minister, or in the long run even to preach, because they are in bondage to their preaching, "a bondage fashioned of exclusive reliance on it for definition and justification of self and of vocation."

The absence of freedom is also reflected in *underinvestment* in preaching. Here, preaching is resisted because intense involvement in any particular expression of ministry invests it with an ultimacy that no human expression, no matter how excellent, can justifiably claim. The minister takes particular note of the limitations of preaching, and is suspicious of claims for its effectiveness. By protecting the ultimate reality from the impurities and the false claims made for particular expressions of ministry, this form of bondage is "like that of the child who comes to feel himself assured of being on the same side as his parents by internalizing their standards and enforcing them, on himself and on others." In this way, parental disfavor and personal failure are avoided. While the minister under the former type of bondage "is preoccupied because satisfactory performance supports his feeling of well-being," the minister under the second type

is more likely to be anxiously forestalling poor performance. He identifies with the ultimate values and criteria by imposing them, in advance, on his own behavior. The impossible ideal of an absolutely perfect sermon is too much before him, and he cannot venture a word without recognizing how far short he falls. So too he is particularly alerted to the disapproval of his hearers, or perhaps their fawning approval for what he knows all too well are the wrong reasons.

There is a third type of attitude toward preaching that avoids these two forms of bondage. This is reflected in the minister who

> throws himself into his preaching—or any other activity—with all the vigor and enthusiasm and verve of the first, "hot" captive above. But he knows just as well as the second, "cool" captive how wrong and partial it can be. So he is as free to abandon or correct or try again his preaching as he is to venture it.

This freedom is akin to that of the child who acts with genuine autonomy because freedom is based on a secure foundation of trust:

> This minister finds his self and his vocation centered, assured, and justified, on some reliable basis. This leaves him freed from the need to find his justification either by exclusive and blind reliance on a particular form of preaching or by the elusive and yearning search for an immediate and direct encounter with the saving and directing ultimate truth.

The assurance that one is already justified is a basis for trust and confidence, enabling free investment in one's preaching. With self and vocation already validated, one does not need to place trust in the precise wording of sermons or in evidence that the message has been appropriated in the way it was intended.

Dittes illustrates how such freedom is reflected in one's preaching method. This illustration draws on the experience of the child who is beginning to exercise personal autonomy. Thus, investment in preaching is analogous to the risk involved in climbing out on a tree limb. Autonomous preaching does not rely on the following devices: (1) *the guaranteed soft landing,* or preaching with abandon because one's self-confidence and vocation derive from competence in some role other than preaching; (2) *clinging to the guaranteed limb,* or making one's preaching fail-safe by such tactics as imitation of one's homiletics professor and preaching the sermons of well-known preachers; (3) *freedom as obligation,* or going out on a limb in a spirit of grim determination to assert one's freedom to say what one wants to say whatever the repercussions.

Genuine freedom in preaching occurs when the minister goes out on a limb, not in spite of the possibility that it may break off but because of it. Such preaching recognizes that (4) *assurance is in the breaking.* In risking failure, the minister discovers the ground of trust. Thus, he

> is free to throw himself unreservedly into his preaching not because he feels confident of being spared catastrophe if the sermon fails but because he has the confidence that maturity of faith and self and ministry—for himself and for his congregation —lies in working through the catastrophe. He fully develops his insights with all the energy and verve and resources and talents he can muster and hopes the congregation can respond in equal freedom. In this encounter may be disaster, and beyond the disaster, growth.

This freedom is not like the expectation that one's parents will always forestall failure (the guaranteed soft landing), or the successful internalization of parents' standards and modes of behavior (the guaranteed limb), or the sense that one's parents *require* spontaneous self-expression (freedom as obligation). It is based on the fact that personal and vocational growth occurs in working through one's failures (assurance is in the breaking).

Dittes illustrates this autonomy by telling the story of a minister who "went out on a limb" in his sermon one Sunday by providing textual "proofs" that God was acting in the events of Pentecost. When some parishioners challenged his "proofs" (and jokingly added some of their own that were only slightly more ludicrous), the minister acknowledged that he had allowed his enthusiasm to exceed his better judgment. The next Sunday his sermon explored his underlying motivations for preaching the previous week's sermon. He said it was possible that he had tried to "prove" God's actions in the Pentecost events because he sees so little concrete evidence of God's power in the church today. But he felt that a more likely explanation was that his earlier sermon reflected "the earnestness of his own conviction that the church is God's, combined with the frustration he felt in stating this clearly and convincingly to the congregation." He felt that his second sermon did make this point clearly and forcefully, but he doubted whether it would have had this effect if it had not been preceded by the earlier sermon in which his chosen limb proved incapable of sustaining him. Thus, his earlier sermon had been a "living parable" of the Pentecost events. The early Christians also went out on a limb, accepting the jibes of less friendly observers, and this very freedom to take risks was itself evidence of God's power.

What is the value of the psychological study of preaching? What is its contribution to the relation between preaching and pastoral counseling? Its major contribution is that it deals with the role of preaching *methods,* especially in shaping relationships with parishioners. Jackson notes that the congregation responded quite differently to different preaching methods, and Dittes notices that a pastor's freedom in the pulpit was directly reflected in parishioners' freedom in the narthex. While ministers may assume that their parishioners respond to sermons in the same way week after week, regardless of the preaching method used, the Jackson study shows that self-conscious changes in preaching method can make a considerable difference in the listeners' response. Dittes' study also suggests that the attitudes of preachers will indirectly communicate their understanding of the Christian gospel. Is the Christian gospel binding and restricting, or does it involve freedom and risk? Is genuine witness to the Christian gospel characterized by reckless abandon, or by self-abandonment? In communicating the gospel, a preacher's attitudes speak more loudly than words.

The major weakness of this approach is that it does not deal directly with the relation between preaching and pastoral counseling. While group dynamics and developmental theories can be used in pastoral counseling, neither Jackson nor Dittes explores the implications of his analysis of preaching methods for counseling. Jackson's distinction between repressive-inspirational and analytical methods of preaching and Dittes' four preaching attitudes would be useful, for example, in evaluating different types of attitudes among pastoral counselors.

Methods in Preaching and Pastoral Counseling

Our assessments of these three approaches to the relation between preaching and pastoral counseling have a common theme. They point to the fact that methods are the major stumbling block in the effort to show that preaching and pastoral counseling are two foci of an integrated ministry. The first approach says virtually nothing about the counseling method on which it is based. The second approach establishes that preaching and pastoral counseling have a common theological foundation. But this theological integration is vitiated when distinctions are made between preaching methods based on verbal communication and pastoral counseling methods based on relationship. The third approach has implications for pastoral counseling methods, but these are not spelled out. This failure to integrate at the point of methods means that we have not progressed much beyond the view, expressed by Edgar Jackson in 1961, that preaching methods are directive while pastoral counseling methods are nondirective.

Chapter 2

The Sermon
and the
Counseling Session

What do preaching and pastoral counseling methods have in common? A good approach to this question is to identify similarities in the sermon and the counseling session. Admittedly, we do not normally think of the sermon and the counseling session as similar. They are considered quite different types of ministerial acts. The sermon is public, the counseling session is private. The sermon is delivered to a congregation, the counseling session involves ministry to as few as one parishioner. The sermon regularly occurs on Sunday morning. The counseling session is specially arranged. The list of differences could go on and on. Are there any similarities at all? An important similarity, often unrecognized, is that both the sermon and the counseling session have a *formal* structure. When the minister enters the pulpit to deliver the sermon, the congregation expects to be spoken to for a reasonably predictable period of time. When pastor and parishioner set up a counseling session, they expect to talk together for about an hour and then take their leave of each other. In both cases, the participants have a pretty good idea of what they expect of each other. During the sermon, the congregation remains silent while the preacher talks. During the counseling session, pastor and parishioner converse with each other.

To say that sermons and counseling sessions have formal structures in common may not seem an important similarity until we consider the extent to which ministry is not formally structured. Much ministry is informal and spontaneous—the casual conversation in the narthex of the church, the urgent telephone call that interrupts the dinner hour, refereeing an argument between organist and choir director. The formally structured act of ministry is the exception, not the rule. That the sermon and counseling session have this formal structure in common, then, is a significant similarity.

But are they similar only in that both are formally structured or do these formal structures also have common features?

Do the sermon and counseling session have similar patterns? If so, can the basic elements of these patterns be identified? I believe they can, and the rest of this chapter is intended to do this. I will begin with the basic elements of the counseling session and then show that sermons typically include the same structural elements.

Elements of the Counseling Session

In my earlier book, *Pastoral Care: A Thematic Approach*, I suggested that the counseling session consists of four elements: (1) identification of the problem; (2) reconstruction of the problem; (3) diagnostic interpretation; (4) pastoral intervention.[16] Brief descriptions of these elements follow:

1. *Identification of the counselee's problem.* The first stage of the counseling session involves identifying the problem that has brought the counselee to the pastor for help. Much pastoral counseling theory focuses on this stage because identification of the counselee's real problem is not always easy. The counselee may be reluctant to discuss the problem until it is clear that the pastor will be understanding. Or the counselee may be willing to open up but may not have a clear idea of what the "real" problem is. Or the counselee may lack the necessary experience in verbalizing personal problems and may need help in learning how to be a "good" counselee. Whatever the reasons for the difficulty in "getting at" the

counselee's problem, the first stage of the session involves identifying this problem.

2. *Reconstruction of the problem.* The second stage explores the various facets of the problem. Ordinarily, this involves discovering what caused the problem to assume its present form and how it is currently being experienced. In other words, the problem is placed in a meaningful context. Typically, this is the longest and most involved stage. The counselor does considerable listening; verbal communication by the counselor is designed to clarify the counselee's story. The counselor's major concern here is to gain a clear understanding of the problem. This stage is complete, therefore, when the counselor feels that such understanding has been gained and the counselee appears persuaded that this is the case.

Pastoral counseling theories emphasize the counselor's role as listener and clarifier. Perhaps because ministers have a rather natural tendency to talk, these theories place considerable emphasis on the task of listening. In fact, listening is emphasized so much that one could gain the erroneous impression that pastoral counseling is nothing but listening. The third stage makes clear that this is not the case.

3. *Diagnostic interpretation.* Once the counselee's problem has been reconstructed, the session normally proceeds to the diagnostic interpretation stage. Here, one communicates one's understanding of the problem to the counselee, noting its negative and positive features. This communication need not be highly complex or technical. In fact, if there has been genuine understanding in the reconstruction phase, the diagnostic interpretation may appear quite obvious to both counselor and counselee. Also, there need not be an abrupt shift in the relationship of counselor and counselee. It is not as though the preceding stage of reconstruction has involved passive listening and now the counselor suddenly becomes aggressive and authoritarian. Rather, during the reconstruction stage the counselor's listening and clarifying already involved interpretive assessments of the problem. Thus, the

diagnostic interpretation gives a certain formal coherence to the various more partial and tentative interpretations ventured in the earlier reconstruction stage. On the other hand, the diagnostic interpretation is generally put forward with a degree of tentativeness, and the counselee is invited to contribute to it. The counselee may agree with every facet of the counselor's interpretation, or the interpretation may prompt the counselee to offer new information or insights that confirm, clarify, or refute some aspects of it.

4. *Pastoral intervention.* When both counselor and counselee agree that the situation has been accurately assessed, they can move to the fourth stage, pastoral intervention. A plan or strategy is developed to deal with the problem, based on the diagnostic interpretation. This may simply involve setting up another counseling session in which the counselee continues to talk about the problem and to explore personal resources for coping with it. Or it may focus on external resources of various kinds, such as the resources of the church or community. Or it may involve exploring available spiritual resources, including prayer.

The diagnostic interpretation and the pastoral intervention stages are related in a reciprocal way. The diagnostic interpretation influences the selection of the plan of intervention, and the effectiveness of this plan is evidence of the accuracy of the interpretation. If the problem has been accurately interpreted, the counseling session can move quite naturally to the intervention stage. The counselee will know what needs to be done without any prompting from the counselor; or the pastor and the counselee will be able to discuss the various options that are open to the counselee in the light of the diagnostic interpretation. But should the attempt to develop a diagnostic interpretation that is convincing to both pastor and counselee fail, the counselor will not want to formulate an intervention plan until both—especially the counselee—are persuaded that the problem has been accurately interpreted. Some problems contain too many unknowns at the time to enable both counselor and counselee to agree about what action needs to be taken. In these cases, they can develop a plan in which some of these unknowns will be explored and clarified, or a plan that incorporates their understanding that the situation is ambiguous and unclear.

Not every counseling session will follow this pattern. Sometimes a counseling session will terminate at the identification, reconstruction, or diagnostic interpretation stage. At other times, it will move directly into one of the later stages because the preceding ones have been adequately covered in previous counseling or precounseling situations. But if a stage is not included either in the counseling session itself or in extra-counseling contacts between pastor and parishioner, one or both parties will sense that "something was missing" in the way this problem was handled. The most typical mistake is concluding the session at the reconstruction stage. The counselee relates the problem, the counselor listens and clarifies, and then there is an awkward uncertainty about what to do next. What does the counselor do after listening? Often the counselor will say, "Well, I hope it has been helpful to you to talk out your problem. Please feel free to come back if you want to talk about it some more." The counselee is a bit puzzled that this is the conclusion, but is diffident about saying, "Thank you, pastor, but I guess I was expecting something more to come of this." As the counselee goes out the door, however, the pastor may have similar thoughts. "It helped Bill to get some things off his chest. But I wanted to do more. I wanted us to do more. Why did it just wind down at the end?" This pastor needs to get these words firmly in mind—"diagnose" and "intervene."

Also, the four elements often fuse into one another. Identification of the problem may not be possible until considerable reconstruction has already occurred. The line between reconstruction and diagnostic interpretation is often blurred and the intervention may already be implicit in the diagnostic interpretation. Thus, division of the four stages is to some extent arbitrary. The counseling session is a fluid process, and the points of transition from stage to stage may be exceedingly difficult to determine. Nonetheless, the one constant is that the stages assume this basic order. Identification of the problem precedes reconstruction; reconstruction precedes the diagnostic interpretation; and the diagnostic interpretation precedes the intervention. Counseling that takes up the stages in a different order or skips stages altogether loses its effectiveness. A session that moves immediately from identifying the problem to intervention, bypassing the stages of reconstruction and diagnostic interpretation, typically results in the counselee's rejection of the plan. It fails to take the unique circumstances of the problem into account. Thus, the stages need to be taken up in the order indicated. In cases where a stage is omitted because it has been handled outside the counseling session, verbal acknowledgment that this stage has been covered in another context is useful. This way both counselor and counselee indicate their awareness that this stage is not simply being neglected.

Elements of the Sermon

The sermon has similar structural elements. In discussing them, I will be arguing that the sermon has a basic structure that cuts beneath specific types of sermons such as expository, topical, or counseling. Undoubtedly, this structure is reflected better in certain types of preaching than in others. At this point, I simply want to establish that the sermon and the counseling session have similar structures; that the sermon, too, consists of the same four structural elements.

I would make one important disclaimer. In noting these structural similarities, I am not suggesting that the sermon is simply an act of counseling. I am not making a case for Fosdick's view that preaching is counseling. By noting these structural similarities, I do not mean to subsume the one form of ministry under the other. On the contrary, the analysis proposed here avoids this very thing. The sermon remains a sermon, with its unique objectives, and the counseling session remains a counseling session, with its own particular objectives. The sermon is not a counseling session and the counseling session is not a preaching event. I am simply claiming that the two structures are remarkably similar.

But what about the terms used to describe this structure (problem, reconstruction, diagnostic interpretation, and intervention)? Do they not have psychotherapeutic connotations? In discussing these stages in counseling, I tried to use these terms in a broader sense. This is especially true of the terms "reconstruction" and "diagnosis." Reconstruction could imply a psychoanalytic process of tracing the problem to its origins. I viewed it, however, as placing the problem in a "context of meaning." Diagnosis could mean trying to label the counselee (from the "obsessive-compulsive" of traditional psychiatric diagnosis to the "poor me" of transactional analysis), but I have viewed it as an "interpretive assessment" of the problem. Thus, I am not suggesting that the structures of the sermon and the counseling session are similar because they are rooted in a psychotherapeutic model of human problem-solving. Rather, the terms are used here in their broader, more generic sense.

The following analyses of the sermon structure include examples from sermons by John Wesley, Martin Luther King, Jr., and John Henry Newman. These three were chosen because they represent quite different theological positions and reflect quite different preaching theories.

1. *Identification of the problem.* In the basic sermon, the first task is to identify the problem being addressed. Here, unlike the topical sermon, the problem is not limited to the topical issues of the day (war, inflation, drug abuse, pornography), though it obviously includes these. Here, unlike the counseling sermon, the problem does not simply mean problems of personal concern (death, divorce, child discipline, a meaningless career), though again it obviously includes these. Here, unlike the expository sermon, the problem is not limited to Biblical matters (problems of interpreting an obscure text or of relating the text to contemporary issues) though

again it clearly includes these. As employed here, "problem" is to be understood in a broad, not a narrow sense, in much the same way that pastoral counseling (unlike vocational counseling, marital counseling, or psychiatric counseling) is not defined by the *problems* it deals with, but by the manner in which it deals with them. To illustrate, I will cite examples of sermons that begin by identifying the problem that the sermon is concerned about. John Wesley's sermon "Upon Our Lord's Sermon on the Mount,"[17] begins this way:

> It is scarce possible to express or conceive what multitudes of souls run on to destruction, because they would not be persuaded to walk in a *narrow* way, even though it were the way to everlasting salvation. And the same thing we may still observe daily. Such is the folly and madness of mankind, that thousands of men still rush on in the way to hell, only because it is a *broad* way. They walk in it themselves, because others do: because so many perish, they will add to the number. Such is the amazing influence of example over the weak, miserable children of men! It continually peoples the regions of death, and drowns numberless souls in everlasting perdition.

Based on Christ's warning to beware of false prophets who come in sheep's clothing but inwardly are ravenous wolves (Matt. 7:15), this sermon quickly identifies the problem. Many are on a course that can only lead to destruction because they are being misled by the words and example of others.

Martin Luther King's sermon "Transformed Nonconformist" is concerned with essentially the same problem but expresses it in much different language.[18] Based on Paul's instruction to Christians that they not be conformed to this world but be transformed by the renewing of their minds (Rom. 12:2), it begins:

> "Do Not Conform" is difficult advice in a generation when crowd pressures have unconsciously conditioned our minds and feet to move to the rhythmic drumbeat of the status quo. Many voices and forces urge us to choose the path of least resistance,

and bid us never to fight for an unpopular cause and never to be found in a pathetic minority of two or three.

Here the problem addressed is the fact that, while Paul counsels against conformity, the contemporary world conditions us to conform to what the majority does.

John Henry Newman's sermon "Love, the One Thing Needful"[19] is based on Paul's observation that if he speaks with the tongues of men and of angels, but has not love, he is like sounding brass or a tinkling cymbal (I Cor. 13:1). It begins:

> I suppose the greater number of persons who try to live Christian lives, and who observe themselves with any care, are dissatisfied with their own state on this point, viz., that, whatever their religious attainments may be, yet they feel that their motive is not the highest—that the love of God, and of man for His sake, is not their ruling principle. They may do much, nay, if it so happen, they may suffer much; but they have little reason to think that they love much, that they do and suffer for love's sake. I do not mean that they thus express themselves exactly, but that they are dissatisfied with themselves, and that when this dissatisfaction is examined into, it will be found ultimately to come to this, though they will give different accounts of it.

Here, the problem is that Christians are dissatisfied with themselves because even the good things that they do are not motivated by their love of God and love of man for God's sake.

It is not too difficult to identify the problem in these three sermons. In two of them, King's and Newman's, this problem is intimated in the title of the sermon. The chosen Scripture text is also a clue. In all three cases, the problem has been identified by the conclusion of the first paragraph. On the other hand, some sermons are similar to counseling sessions in which the problem is not immediately self-evident. A good example of this is a sermon by Austin Farrer, entitled "Caprice," which deals with the Old Testament story of Ruth and Naomi.[20] It begins:

> Mothers-in-law have had a bad press on the whole, but Ruth was devoted to hers. That is, whether she was devoted in feeling, I do not know, but on the day when Naomi emigrated Ruth devoted herself to her in fact; and, after that, she was devoted in the literal sense—she had sworn away her liberty, she had committed herself.

This opening paragraph gives a vague indication that the sermon is not about mothers-in-law but about the problem of commitment. However, not until the third paragraph do we discover that the sermon is about commitment that is random, quixotic, irrational, and capricious. The beginning paragraph prepares the listener for this and there is certainly no disjuncture between this paragraph and the rest of the sermon. But one would miss much of the subtlety of the sermon if one concluded that this will simply be another sermon about the solid virtues of commitment. The sermon deals with the capricious character of religious commitment. Thus, as in counseling, so also in the sermon, the problem may not be immediately evident. The general problem area may be fairly clear from the outset, but the preacher (no less than the counselee) may take a rather circuitous route in arriving at the precise nature of the problem being addressed.

2. *Reconstruction of the problem.* The second stage is the reconstruction of the problem. In the sermon, as in the counseling session, this involves placing the problem in a meaningful context. In his sermon on the dangers of following those who mislead us, Wesley explains what a false prophet is, itemizes the subtle devices that false prophets use to deceive the unwary, and proposes guidelines by which false prophets can be identified. In his sermon on nonconformity, King first discusses the fact that Christians have a mandate to be nonconformist, then enumerates some of the specific pressures that the contemporary world exerts on people to conform, then reflects that conformity is particularly evident in the church, "an institution which has often served to crystallize, conserve, and even bless the patterns of majority opinion." In his sermon on the failure of Christians to act

from the motivation of love, Newman identifies signs of the absence of love in the life of the Christian, including substituting obedience for love, expressing remorse but lacking genuine repentance, becoming engrossed in the novelties and excitement of religion, and losing one's religious convictions when confronted with affliction.

These brief summaries fail to do justice to the richness and complexity of these reconstructions, but they show that the sermon has a reconstruction phase in which the preacher elaborates on the reasons why the problem exists and why it is important to consider, or explores various facets of the problem. The reconstruction may consist primarily of insights into the nature of the problem provided by Scripture, as in the case of Wesley, or may involve analysis of contemporary man, as in the case of King, or may employ both Scriptural and contemporary analysis, as in the case of Newman. Either is a legitimate way of reconstructing the problem. Indeed, there are parallels to these two approaches in the pastoral counseling setting. One counselee may understand a personal problem in the light of insights gained from the Bible or Christian tradition, another will understand the problems in terms of the social and personal pressures of contemporary life, and a third will use a combination of the two. The *third* stage of the sermon, however, is invariably informed by Scripture or Christian tradition. Rarely is it based solely on insights derived from observation of contemporary life.

3. *The diagnostic interpretation.* The diagnostic interpretation in the sermon is an interpretive assessment of the problem in the light of the preceding reconstruction. Normally it cuts to the heart of the matter. It sizes up the whole problem in an incisive way, typically by means of Biblical or theological understandings.

In Wesley's sermon, the diagnostic interpretation comes at the conclusion of the reconstruction stage. It centers on the existence of false prophets in the church, and the difficult dilemma in which this places the average Christian. Wesley acknowledges that one could conclude from what he has been saying about false prophets that they are so dangerous that we should not listen to them at all. He confesses that this is an attractive response, but one that he has finally rejected on the grounds that, in Jesus' time, the false prophets were the duly appointed teachers in the synagogue. Refusal to hear false prophets could mean the neglect of worship and cutting oneself off from the ordinances of God. As Wesley points out, Christ warns his disciples to beware of false prophets, but does not forbid them to hear these prophets. On the contrary:

> He, in effect, commands them so to do, in those words, "All, therefore, whatsoever they bid you observe, that observe and do": for unless they heard them, they could not know, much less observe, whatsoever they bade them do. Here, then, our Lord Himself gives a plain direction, both to His Apostles and the whole multitude, in some circumstances, to hear even false prophets, known and acknowledged so to be.

Thus, Wesley does not advise people to avoid false prophets altogether. The issue is more complex than that.

After recounting the pressures that society and the church exert on us to conform, King moves into the crux of the issue by pointing out: "Nonconformity in itself, however, may not necessarily be good and may at times possess neither transforming nor redemptive power. Nonconformity per se contains no saving value, and may represent in some circumstances little more than a form of exhibitionism." He then draws attention to Paul's formula for constructive nonconformity.

> Nonconformity is creative when it is controlled and directed by a transformed life and is constructive when it embraces a new mental outlook. By opening our lives to God in Christ we become new creatures. This experience, which Jesus spoke of as the new birth, is essential if we are to be transformed nonconformists and freed from the cold hardheartedness and self-righteousness so often characteristic of nonconformity.

Thus, King's diagnosis focuses on the need for a nonconformity that is constructive, controlled, and directed by a transformed mental outlook.

After discussing the various signs of the absence of love in the life of the Christian, Newman probes the root cause of this deficiency of love toward God and other individuals. In his judgment,

> fanciful though it may appear at first sight to say so, the comforts of life are the main cause of it; and, much as we may lament and struggle against it, till we learn to dispense with them in good measure, we shall not overcome it.

Newman acknowledges that a "hard life" does not guarantee that we will become more loving, but experience of this hard life teaches us that much of what passes for love today is affected and hypocritical. Through genuine suffering and deprivation, one learns to differentiate real expressions of love from their counterfeits. Through personal discomfort, one's love becomes attuned to the real situation and is uncompromising in its moral force.

These diagnostic interpretations are based on the reconstruction that preceded them. Yet, each preacher is aware that his diagnosis is interpretive. It does not follow from the reconstruction in the same ineluctable fashion that the conclusion to a syllogism follows inevitably from the major and minor premises. Wesley, for example, confesses that for many years he had been almost afraid to speak at all concerning the problem of false prophets, "being unable to determine one way or the other, or to give any judgement upon it." Similarly, Newman acknowledges that his diagnosis of the problem may at first sight seem fanciful. Both Wesley and Newman recognize that the diagnosis given is an interpretation.

Recognizing this, they support the diagnosis with a Biblical passage or allusion. Wesley cites Jesus' instructions to his disciples, King cites Paul's distinction between conformity and transformation, and Newman alludes to "what Scripture calls this hypocrisy, which we see around us." Thus, the Scriptures may or may not have been employed in the reconstruction stage of the sermon, but Biblical references are almost invariably involved in the diagnostic interpretation. The authoritative nature of the diagnostic interpretation consists not in its logic, or in the self-confidence of the preacher, but in the fact that it has Scriptural support.

Preachers appear to recognize that their use of Scripture in this way is deliberately selective. In the reconstruction stage, one may use a variety of Scriptural references to identify the complexities of the problem being addressed. But in the diagnostic stage, one tends to focus on a single Biblical affirmation. While this risks the oversimplification of the Christian gospel, the preacher recognizes the greater danger that the diagnosis will lack specificity and directness. Using various Biblical passages to provide different perspectives on the problem introduces diffuseness at a point where precision is required. Thus, the diagnostic interpretation does not explicitly rule out other valid interpretations of the problem. Rather, it puts them aside, much as the counselor may choose to leave aside alternative diagnoses of the problem in order to develop a case for the diagnosis that appears to be most urgently needed.

There are instances when the preacher does not offer a precise diagnosis of the problem. Sometimes the problem is ambiguous and continues to elude human comprehension. An example is Paul Tillich's sermon on "Faith and Uncertainty."[21] In this sermon, Tillich takes up the problem of uncertainty in matters of ultimate concern. In reconstructing the problem, he develops the view that we cannot rid ourselves of uncertainty by means of personal religious experience, theological argument, or the personal reliability of the Biblical writers. He diagnoses the problem of uncertainty, then, as one that will always elude our grasp. But he supports his reluctance to press for greater certainty by noting that the Bible and the confessions of all the great Christian witnesses indicate that we lose our certainty in matters of ultimate concern as soon as we regard it as *our* certainty. Thus, Tillich leaves the problem in essentially the same place that he began, but he has cited a Biblical understanding of faith as justification for the Christian's refusal to attempt to resolve the problem in any definitive way.

4. *Pastoral intervention.* The fourth stage of the sermon deals with the problem as diagnosed. This part typically points beyond the sermon itself by indicating some of the ways the congregation might respond to the problem. These proposed responses grow directly out of the diagnostic interpretation and are the practical evidence of its value. Thus, Wesley has ruled out the possibility that the problem of false prophets can be solved by refusing to attend assemblies whose speakers are presumed to be false prophets. Rather, each individual will simply have to exercise good judgment. As Wesley puts it:

> All, therefore, which I can say is this: In any particular case, wait upon God by humble and earnest prayer, and then act according to the best light you have: act according to what you are persuaded, upon the whole, will be most for your spiritual advantage.

Thus, Wesley expects individuals to pray and then act according to their best lights. In addition, one can test what is being proclaimed against Biblical passages:

> Believe nothing they say, unless it is clearly confirmed by passages of holy writ. Wholly reject whatsoever differs therefrom, whatever is not confirmed thereby. And, in particular, reject, with the utmost abhorrence, whatsoever is described as the way of salvation, that is either different from, or short of, the way our Lord has marked out in the foregoing discourse.

Acknowledging that he cannot provide a foolproof method for avoiding the dangers of false prophets, Wesley nonetheless suggests some things that his listeners can do to protect themselves. One can make prayerful assessment of the effects of the speaker's words on one's spiritual condition.

One can also check the speaker's words against the Scriptures. Furthermore, Wesley encourages special wariness when the speaker is describing the way of salvation.

The fourth stage of King's sermon calls for "a dedicated circle of transformed nonconformists." In challenging his listeners to join this circle, King stresses the cost and pain involved in being part of the cadre of individuals who are "creatively maladjusted" to a decadent society. To be a Christian means to carry one's cross until "that very cross leaves its marks upon us and redeems us to that more excellent way which comes only through suffering." This dedicated circle of transformed nonconformists will be known not by their exhibitionism but by their acceptance of the "more excellent way" of suffering.

In his intervention, Newman recommends cultivating "a constant sense of the love of your Lord and Savior in dying on the cross for you." He calls on his listeners to think of the cross when they rise in the morning and when they go to bed at night, when they go out and come in, when they buy and when they sell, and when they labor and when they rest. Through such thoughts, one will begin to develop the self-discipline necessary to act in love toward others.

Undoubtedly, the interventions recommended in these three sermons are not the only appropriate responses to the problem. The listener may be able to conceive of alternative responses. The preacher, in other sermons, may propose different ways of responding to this problem, even when the diagnosis is similar. But the possibility of alternative responses to the problem does not invalidate these particular proposals as long as they grow directly out of the diagnosis. In the three sermons discussed, the recommended interventions are consistent with the diagnoses. For Wesley, the problem of false prophets is complex and cannot be solved by avoiding such individuals altogether. So his recommended intervention centers on certain tests (experiential and Scriptural) that the listener can use to evaluate the proclamation of any speaker. King diagnoses the problem of conformity as the malady of a decadent society, so his intervention challenges his listeners to join in the small minority willing to suffer in creative nonconformity. Newman attributes the absence of love to the fact that his listeners have not suffered enough. So, in the intervention stage of the sermon, he advocates a constant reflection on the sufferings of Christ.

In all three cases, the recommended intervention is based on the diagnostic interpretation. In each case, the intervention is a specific response to the diagnosis; it is not a set of vague generalities. Because it grows so directly out of the diagnostic interpretation, the diagnostic stage has particular importance. The diagnostic interpretation makes the transition from understanding to action. This makes it the major factor in the sermon's effectiveness. Perhaps preachers intuitively sense its importance when they have recourse to the Scriptures to support this interpretation. All three sermons stressed the Biblical basis of the diagnostic interpretation. This is rather remarkable when we consider that the three preachers differ quite markedly in their theological viewpoints, their attitudes toward the Bible, and their theories of preaching.

Austin Farrer's "In Season and Out"

Thus far, I have used excerpts from three sermons to illustrate that the sermon and the counseling session have similar structures. I now want to look at an entire sermon and show how it reflects these four stages. Analyzing an entire sermon enables us to see how each stage builds on the preceding one. It also enables us to compare the sermon and counseling session structures. While the counseling session and the sermon usually differ in length (most sermons do not last an hour), the relative length of each stage of the process is quite similar in the two structures. Generally speaking, the identification of the problem is relatively brief, the reconstruction of the problem is the longest stage of the four, and the diagnostic interpretation varies in length according to the complexity of the problem. The intervention stage is seldom as long as the reconstruction stage, but usually longer than the first stage.

The sermon chosen to illustrate these structural similarities is Austin Farrer's "In Season and Out."[22] It was preached to a student congregation at Oxford University shortly after a special mission conducted by an archbishop and a Franciscan monk. I have divided the sermon into four stages, with brief interpretive comments following each section. The first section of the sermon consists of four rather brief paragraphs that identify the basic problem.

Stage 1: Identification of the Problem

Someone has just said to me, "I hope you saw the effect of the mission in your early Chapel this morning." "Yes, certainly," I replied, "the congregation was down by a third." "Oh," said my interlocutor, "that's not the answer I expected." "Maybe not," said I, "but it was the result that I anticipated."

I am not repeating this scrap of conversation to show you how clever I am, for it does not take a very brilliant mind to draw the moral from a striking experience half-a-dozen times repeated; and half-a-dozen missions have come and gone, while I have been sitting here.

Why then, in heaven's name, do we have missions? It may well be asked, and the best answer I can give, is that the long-term result is less negative than the immediate effect. But for the moment I am all out to depress you, and it is the immediate effect on which I will turn your eyes.

Perhaps we can get some light on the matter from a parable of Christ, so short and so bare, that it hardly attracts the reader's attention. A man who had a job of hard work to be done, told his two sons to go and do it. "With pleasure," said the one, and did nothing about it. "Hell, no," said the other, or words to that effect, and went and did it. The obvious moral of the story is that deeds are more important than words; but there is a further moral, less obvious—that people have an ineradicable tendency to substitute words for deeds.

The negative effect of missions on regular chapel attendance is an example of a more perennial problem, i.e., that *people have a tendency to substitute words for deeds.* Farrer's acquaintance thought that the mission, which inspired students to make verbal commitments to the faith, would issue in concrete acts of devotion. Then why did the mission have the opposite effect? Christ's parable of the two sons offers a clue because it deals with our tendency to substitute words for deeds. The first son makes a verbal commitment but fails to carry it through with concrete acts. The second son carries through on the deed, but not from a prior verbal commitment.

As used here, the parable not only illustrates the problem but contributes to identifying it. The problem is not identified as the difficulty of choosing between competing opportunities to make religious affirmations (mission vs. morning chapel), but as the more fundamental tendency to substitute words for deeds.

Thus, the issue with which the reconstruction stage of the sermon will be concerned is not the problem of choosing between two valuable religious activities, or some other problem relating to the mission and its impact on students, but on the more fundamental problem of our tendency to substitute talk for action. This reconstruction begins by exploring Christ's parable of the two sons in greater depth.

Stage 2: Reconstruction of the Problem

Christ's parables are natural stories—they do not need a lot of special assumptions to explain them. That means, in the present case, that we are not to make up a whole novel about the distinct and opposed characters of the two young men, or of how they got to be the way that they were. They are just sons, and we know what sons are like. They have a reluctant regard for the old man, and a certain sense of decency in face of his demands, but then they detest being ordered about, or dropping their own ploys to pick up his. Furthermore, they are brothers, as well as being sons; and that means that whatever line the elder takes, the younger will take the other line. Each has a negative and positive reaction towards his father's wishes, and each gives expression to both reactions. The first expresses loyalty in words, and reluctance in deeds; the second reluctance in words, and loyalty in deeds. They both get everything out of their systems, which is no doubt very satisfactory from the point of view of their emotional health—only one does the job and the other doesn't. The difference may be psychologically trivial, but it has some practical bearing, the father is bound to feel.

The brothers differed in the immediate impact of their father on them. The first was a really nice lad, inclined to smile and say "Yes." The idea of pleasing his father was agreeable. The negative wave of reluctance did not rise, until the effort of putting on boots, and getting the hoe, brought home to him what a bore it would be. The other was a horrid boy: his father simply irritated him. The negative wave came straight up, and broke in his father's face. But it had broken, and he went off in full reaction, feeling there was something to be put right and that only one thing would put it right, a spell with the hoe.

Now you think I am all out to scold you, but here is a surprise for you. I do not think you are at all like this horrid youth. When a mission is preached by a great and dedicated man, his words come home with the force of divine love. God speaks, and your reaction to your heavenly father is kind and amiable. You are not at all inclined to say "Hell, no!"—especially when the spoken word is reinforced by the word clothed in flesh and blood, the living sermon of a Franciscan in our midst, a man who has done what the apostles did, and given up all for the special service of Christ. These things move you, and you take some immediate trouble, perhaps, to interest your friends in what you find holy and good.

Then comes the reaction. We have shot off our religious sentiments. We owe ourselves an amusing Saturday night, and a Sunday morning in bed. It was natural, saying "Yes" to an Archbishop and a Franciscan: they both had very nice voices. It is equally natural saying "No" to an alarm-clock: its voice is not agreeable at all, nor is the prospect of slushy snow on the ground outside. We forget that what makes a Franciscan a Franciscan is a habit of getting up at five o'clock no matter what, doing all the menial work that others do for us, and himself looking after what profane lips call the most god-forsaken specimens of the human race.

In the bad old days between the two wars, the capitalist nations endured a boom-and-bust economic rhythm, which was accepted as a kind of fate. It was chastening to reflect, as you went into the boom, that over-production would produce the inevitable slump; and heartening to remember, when several million of your countrymen were out of work, that they would not have to starve or idle for more than a year or two, before the compensating boom began slowly to gather momentum. As in *laissez-faire* economics, so in "go-as-you-please" love affairs, and friendships, too; the boom-and-bust rhythm keeps rocketing to extremes. You think your relationship lies in ruins after the row of last night? Cheer up: "the falling-out of faithful friends renewing is of love." You have both worked off your negative emotions in the most satisfactory manner; now is the time for a really juicy reconciliation. And perhaps you had better try to forget (since it would spoil the purity of your emotion) that love-feasts produce satiety and renewed confidences lead to further estrangements.

In reconstructing the problem, Farrer notes that the attitudes of each son in the parable alternate between positive and negative. In the long run, the psychological difference in the way they responded to their father's request may be negligible. But, in the shorter run, the difference has a practical bearing on the problem of our tendency to substitute words for deeds. One son acted while the other did not. To the father who wants the work in the fields done, this practical difference is significant.

Building on this practical difference in the sons' responses to their father's request, Farrer continues with more careful scrutiny of the attitudes reflected in their behavior. He focuses most on the attitude of the first son because it more nearly parallels the case with which he began (the effect of the mission on chapel attendance) and the problem he wants to address (the failure of words to issue into action). Here, an initially positive sentiment is soon exhausted and the reaction sets in, with the deeds they originally inspired failing to materialize. This pattern of positive feelings followed by a negative reaction is no different from the alternating rhythm of laissez-faire economics or stormy love affairs, neither of which are notable for their stability.

The reconstruction involves clarifying the attitudes that underlie our tendency to substitute words for deeds. The basic reason we fail to carry our words into deeds is that we are subject to the same alternation of positive and negative attitudes reflected in the parable.

The diagnostic interpretation stage provides an assessment of what is wrong with this alternating pattern and draws attention to the resources that are available for doing something about it. It begins with a critique of the alternating pattern in love relationships:

Stage 3: The Diagnostic Interpretation

Where people are childish enough, and where their emotional rhythms are in tune, I suppose they may go on like this for a life-time. Quarrelling is a sort of relationship, and anything is better than indifference. Yet they are surely happiest in this kind of life, who live in the moment, and manage not to look before or after. It is better to do this sort of thing, than to know that this sort of thing is what you do.

Especially when the relationship in question is with your Creator, for, to begin with, you cannot get him to play this game with you: his is an unchanging love. Christ is the same today, yesterday and for ever.

Far more serious characters than you or I have confessed a humiliating alternation of moods in their religion:

Oh, to vex me, contraries meet in one;
Inconstancy unnaturally hath begot
A constant habit; that when I would not
I change in vows, and in devotion.
As humorous is my contrition
As my profane Love, and as soon forgot;
As riddlingly distemper'd, cold and hot,

As praying, as mute; as infinite, as none.
I durst not view heaven yesterday; and today
In prayers, and flattering speeches I court God:
Tomorrow I quake with true fear of His rod.
So my devout fits come and go away
Like a fantastic Ague: save that here
Those are my best days, when I shake with fear.

The difference between Dr Donne and us, is that when he was off God, he was frightened of him, and we manage not to be. The same author prays in his *Litany,* "That we may change to evenness this intermittent aguish Piety"; that is, this recurrent malaria of a religion. And certainly that is the task: not to have booms and slumps, whether over a mission or over anything else, but to go on steadily in a tranquil and loving obedience to God. But how? Perhaps—if I dare suggest to you anything so unromantic—we may get some light on the matter by observing the difference between steady marriages and exciting love-affairs.

The difference to which I will call attention is a difference in the expression of the positive emotion. In love-affairs, it tends to get expressed in common pleasures; in marriage, rather in common enterprises. When the pleasures are over, they are over, and leave the field clear for a reaction. But the common enterprises reach away into the future, and continue to unite us in the pursuit of them. The revolving day brings round its tasks unbidden; common cares mutually endear us, when common delights would only exhaust us.

The diagnostic interpretation begins by noting that the alternation of positive and negative feelings in love relationships is childish and immature. This alternating pattern will not work in religious life. Not only is it psychologically immature but, more important, it is not the way our Creator relates to us. His love is not subject to this same alternating pattern of positive and negative attitudes: "Christ is the same yesterday and today and for ever." Promises are kept. Words result in deeds. How God relates to us is crucial to the sermon's diagnosis of the problem.

This Biblical understanding of the constancy of God's

love, supported by Donne's anguished prayer for such constancy in his own religious life, leads to an incisive diagnostic statement: "And certainly that is the task: not to have booms and slumps . . . but to go on steadily in a tranquil and loving obedience to God. But how?" Farrer answers this question, "But how?" by suggesting that the *positive* emotion is the key factor. The task is to focus on the positive emotion and to explore ways in which it can issue into more enduring commitments.

The steady marriage, however unromantic it may seem, demonstrates that the alternation of positive and negative attitudes is not inevitable if positive sentiments can be directed toward common enterprises and sustained by them. Thus, the reconstruction stage focuses on examples in which positive and negative feelings alternate. In contrast, the diagnostic interpretation cites evidence, also drawn from human relationships, to show that the bondage of alternating emotions can be overcome. Moreover, this example of human interaction *is* positive precisely because it is similar to the way that God relates to us—in love extended through enduring enterprises.

Thus the diagnostic interpretation focuses on the *positive* resources of the individual Christian. It does not dwell on the negative emotion and the means whereby it might be purged, but instead centers on the positive emotion and the means whereby it might be extended. This focus is consistent with Farrer's earlier suggestion that his listeners are more similar to the first son in the parable. The diagnosis is not concerned with eradicating the *negative* emotion ("Hell, no!"), but with extending the *positive* emotion ("I will go"). The issue still unresolved is: How do we ensure that the positive emotion issues in enduring enterprises? If extending the positive emotion is the preferred approach to the problem, what concrete steps can be taken to accomplish this? The fourth stage of the sermon is directed to this very practical question.

Stage 4: Treatment or Intervention

So, then, the worship of the heart is a fine thing, and it would be wretched if we could never delight in God, or enjoy our religion. But our piety must grow into set customs, continuous enterprises in union with God's grace. If in our worship we can dwell with affection on God's goodness, or in prayer on the names of our fellow men, how excellent. But we must form resolutions. Lord, what wilt thou have me to *do?* What does my neighbor need from me? There is no need for resolutions to be original since we are so bad at keeping them. All we often need is to revive them. What they *must* be, is practical and particular: to pray at the hour I had promised, to be at communion on Sunday, to visit the sick friend, to answer the awkward correspondent, *not* to let so-and-so provoke me, to keep proper hours for my work, to avoid my besetting sin.

Here the preacher recommends developing one's positive religious attitudes into set customs of worship and prayer, and into service to friends and others in need. The task is not to conjure up new customs but to revive the old. Also, these customs need to be practical and specific. They should be like the small expressions of faithfulness and reliability that enable participants in the steady marriage to envision common enterprises of an enduring nature. While Farrer mentions various examples of such customs, his main concern is for establishing a continuing pattern of activity, not one that waits for extraordinary circumstances but one that, like the steady marriage, centers on recurrent and predictable claims on one's time and energy. Most important, the proposals offered in this section of the sermon are squarely based on the diagnostic interpretation in their emphases on the cultivation of positive intentions. Because this is the case, they reinforce this interpretation.

It is safe to conclude that Farrer's sermon includes all four stages. Some readers may disagree with our divisions. Frequently, the point of transition from one stage to another is difficult to identify precisely. But what matters is that it was possible to show that the sermon was shaped by these four stages.

Conclusion

My purpose in this chapter has not been to reduce the sermon and counseling session to a simple formula. Certainly, I am not offering preachers a new "guaranteed limb." I simply wanted to identify structural similarities in the sermon and counseling session as a step toward integrating preaching and pastoral counseling. If this were a historical study, one might trace these structural similarities to a period in the development of the Christian ministry when preaching and pastoral counseling were more nearly integrated than they are now. Since this is not a historical study, I am content merely to draw attention to these similarities. However, they do prompt us to ask whether, as preachers on the one hand and counselors on the other, our singleminded attention to the theories and techniques of our own disciplines has caused us to overlook some fairly obvious similarities in these two forms of ministry.

Chapter 3

Theological Diagnosis in Pastoral Counseling

The most important structural link between preaching and pastoral counseling is the diagnostic interpretation. The other three structural elements are obviously important, but I would contend that diagnostic interpretation is the primary basis for the similarity between these two forms of ministry. It would probably not be accurate to say that this diagnostic element is shared only by preaching and pastoral counseling among the various expressions of ministry, but it *is* the case that preaching and pastoral counseling accord diagnosis a central importance that is not typical of other expressions of ministry.

Henri Nouwen identifies these as basic expressions of ministry: teaching, preaching, individual pastoral care, organizing, and celebrating.[23] It is almost self-evident that the *essential* characteristic of teaching, organizing, and celebrating is not diagnosis. Diagnosis of problems may be an important feature of these expressions of ministry, but there are many situations in which teaching, organizing, and celebrating can occur without a diagnostic element. The same is not true of preaching and pastoral counseling. As we saw in the preceding chapter, sermons and pastoral counseling sessions necessarily include a diagnostic element. Without this element, neither the sermon nor the counseling session can effect a transition from understanding to action. In both cases, it is vitally important to their effectiveness that this transition occur.

Diagnosis in Pastoral Counseling

There is little reference to "diagnosis" in current theories of pastoral counseling. What reference there is to diagnosis is mainly negative. The reason for this is not difficult to identify. Since the 1950's, the dominant counseling theory in pastoral counseling has been the client-centered approach. Its attractiveness to pastoral counselors was due in part to its rejection of the medical aura of psychoanalysis. Client-centered therapists made no claim to psychiatric expertise and rejected the view that counseling is similar to medical diagnosis. In their view, the task of psychotherapy is not to trace the history of the counselee's problem as one would explore the etiology of an illness, but to focus on the counselee's current experience. The counselee may voluntarily talk about past experiences, including early childhood experiences, but in the client-centered view this material from the past is important only as it is currently experienced.

By rejecting the idea that counseling is like tracing the etiology of an illness, client-centered therapy appeared to eliminate the notion of diagnosis. When counseling is not interested in tracing a problem back to its origins, the term "diagnosis" no longer seems appropriate. Thomas Oden points out that instead of emphasizing special adeptness in diagnostic training, Carl Rogers

> has described effective therapy essentially in terms of a relationship in which one enters into the sufferer's frame of reference, empathetically participating with him in his struggle to understand himself, clarifying his feelings and the alternatives that he sees for himself. Unlike psycho-analysis, which involves an advanced diagnostic ability that can only be the fruit of extensive training, client-centered therapy has proven itself easily adaptable by pastors and priests in the pastoral situation.[24]

Thus, the language of empathetic understanding, of listening and clarifying, replaced the earlier language of diagnosis. The term "diagnosis" went out of favor, and little has been done in recent years to reverse this. Even critics of client-centered therapy have rarely criticized its attitude toward diagnosis. Their criticisms have been directed toward its other features. The influence of client-centered therapy on pastoral counseling, then, has been responsible for the absence of diagnosis.

However, it can be argued that diagnosis has always been an important part of client-centered therapy. We need not go to psychoanalytic theory to recover the diagnostic element in pastoral counseling. Moreover, it is inaccurate to talk about the "recovery" of the diagnostic element, as though it has been eliminated from pastoral counseling. In good client-centered counseling, this diagnostic element has continued to exist in spite of the fact that pastoral counseling theories based on client-centered principles have neglected it. This neglect is due largely to the tendency of pastoral counselors to limit the meaning of the word "diagnosis" to the medical understanding of the term. But, as I will show in a moment, Carl Rogers developed a different conception of the term "diagnosis," and this understanding has continued to inform effective pastoral counseling even though the term itself has not been used.

Diagnosis in Preaching

About the same time that client-centered therapy became influential in pastoral counseling, the view that preaching is basically proclamation became the dominant preaching theory. Preaching based on this model emphasizes the preacher's task of declaring the good news of the gospel. As Oden puts it: "The purpose of proclamation is that of calling man to an awareness of the reality of the situation in which he already exists."[25] The proclamatory sermon makes declarative statements, especially with regard to God's self-disclosure in Jesus Christ. The sermon "witnesses" to this self-disclosure, and the listener is challenged to "hear" this witness and respond to this reality.

In this view of preaching, one's role is to *declare,* not *diagnose.* Announcing the good news of God's self-disclosure in Jesus Christ is not a diagnostic activity. Thus, Oden believes that Carl Rogers, with his rejection of "special adeptness in diagnostic training" and his emphasis on the counselor's empathetic participation in "the sufferer's frame of reference," has "most meaningfully spelled out an understanding of therapy relevant to Christian proclamation."[26] Like client-centered counseling, proclamatory preaching docs not require "special adeptness in diagnostic training." It simply requires one to announce the good news of the gospel.

However, if effective pastoral counseling continues to employ a modified form of diagnosis, we may ask whether the effective proclamatory sermon also retains a modified form of diagnosis? Good proclamatory sermons make significant use of diagnostic interpretation, as is illustrated by the sermons Karl Barth preached to inmates in the prison at Basel.[27] These sermons follow the four stages of the sermon structure. Even more significantly, the proclamation is most decisively expressed in the diagnostic interpretation stage.

For example, in "The Beginning of Wisdom" Barth is concerned with the problem of achieving wisdom. Here he accepts the Biblical view that "the fear of the Lord is the beginning of wisdom." But in his diagnostic interpretation, he observes that the *fear* of the Lord is commonly misunderstood. Many equate it with anxiety. But anxiety is not the beginning, it is the end of wisdom. It reflects an inordinate fear of the terrors of this world and of God, as though he were some kind of "oversized giant prosecutor." These are false fears. Genuine fear of the Lord is the awareness that the gracious, merciful, and redemptive experiences in life are acts of God. Thus, genuine "fear of the Lord" is not anxiety, but awareness:

It is nothing short of a discovery when a man is suddenly confronted with this reality. It is not unlike the experience of Columbus who, sailing out for India, suddenly hit upon the continent of America. *This* I did not know. *This* nobody ever told me. *This* I could never have found out by myself—that God is *this* God, that God does *these* things. Solomon faced this fact, this loving-kindness, these mighty deeds which God accomplished with his people, with his father, David, and with himself. And faced with this wondrous reality, he feared the Lord. Out of this fear he became the wise Solomon.

This statement is, at one and the same time, diagnostic and proclamatory. It is diagnostic in that it discriminates true from false understandings of the meaning of "the fear of the Lord." This fear is not anxiety but awareness that the redemptive experiences of life are acts of God. By distinguishing fear as awareness of God from fear as anxiety about God, Barth renders a diagnostic interpretation of the problem of acquiring wisdom. However, in developing this diagnosis, he also proclaims a reality that already exists. All that we need in order to begin living in wisdom is to become aware that our experiences of grace, mercy, and redemption are acts of God. Thus, for us as for Columbus discovering America, the solution to the problem of wisdom is awareness. One does not strive for wisdom or wait for old age to confer wisdom. Rather, one becomes aware of a reality that already exists, and in that awareness one begins a life of wisdom. The diagnosis of the problem of wisdom and how one acquires it is therefore not complete until it is placed in the context of proclamation. Conversely, the proclamation is persuasive because it is preceded by a critical assessment of false understandings of the meaning of the fear of the Lord. We can conclude that, in this sermon at least, diagnosis and proclamation are virtually inseparable.

Good proclamation preaching does not eliminate the diagnostic interpretation. Rather, it locates this interpretation in the context of proclamation. This means that the problem with which the sermon is concerned is generally diagnosed as one of faulty awareness or perception. In the intervention stage, Barth typically appeals to his listeners to perceive the problem in a new way. While this may seem to severely limit the range of possible resolutions of the problem, we should keep in mind that in many counseling theories, perceiving the problem in new ways is the key to its resolution. (Hiltner calls this "turning the corner" on the problem.) In diagnosing the problem in terms of awareness the proclamatory sermon is fundamentally similar to these "insight" theories.

Another effect of placing the diagnostic interpretation in a proclamatory context is that the diagnosis is necessarily theological. The diagnosis may be informed by psychological insights into human experience, but its cogency derives from Christian affirmations concerning God's nature and activities. Barth's diagnostic interpretation of the fear of God as the beginning of wisdom has its basis in the affirmation that our experiences of grace, mercy, and redemption are acts of God. If this were not the case, his distinction between fear and anxiety would not be compelling.

Diagnostic use of theology in preaching is not unique to the proclamation sermon. But the proclamation sermon's unique use of theology as a diagnostic tool—presenting diagnosis within the context of announcement—invites us to consider the *variety* of ways that preaching employs theology diagnostically. What are some of the different ways that theology functions diagnostically in sermons? Can we identify some of these ways and compare their objectives? These are the questions to which Chapter 4 will be addressed. Our discussion in this chapter continues with the issue of diagnosis in pastoral counseling.

The Rogerian Critique of the Diagnostic Attitude

Let us begin with Carl Rogers' own discussion of diagnosis in counseling.[28] His criticism of diagnosis is based on the fact that client-centered counselors have come to recognize that if we can provide understanding of the way the client seems to himself at this moment, he can do the rest. The therapist must lay aside his preoccupation with diagnosis and his diagnostic shrewdness, must discard his tendency to make professional evaluations, must cease his endeavors to formulate an accurate prognosis, must give up the temptation subtly to guide the individual, and must concentrate on one purpose only; that of providing deep understanding and acceptance of the attitudes consciously held at this moment by the client as he explores step by step into the dangerous areas which he has been denying to consciousness.

By laying aside a preoccupation with diagnosis, the therapist enters into the client's internal frame of reference. Diagnosis implies an external perspective, the perspective of observation rather than participation in the client's own frame of reference. In contrast to diagnosis, empathic understanding and acceptance means entering into the client's own perceptual field.

The difference between entering into the client's own internal frame of reference instead of maintaining an external diagnostic perspective is reflected not in what one says but how one says it. It is a difference of attitude, not language. Rogers points out that a statement that would appear to be empathic can convey a diagnostic attitude. He offers the following hypothetical example as a case in point:

Client: I feel as though my mother is always watching me and criticizing what I do. It gets me all stirred up inside. I try not to let that happen, but you know, there are times when I feel her eagle eye on me that I just boil inwardly.

Counselor: You resent her criticism.

Rogers points out that the statement "you resent her criticism" can come across to the client as either empathic or diagnostic. It will reflect empathic understanding if the counselor's tone of voice carries the implication, "If I understand you correctly, you feel pretty resentful toward her criticism.

Is that right?" It will be perceived as diagnostic if the statement communicates the same attitude that one might have in informing another person that he has the measles or is sitting on one's hat. In the former instance, the reaction of the client is likely to be, "Yes, that is the way I feel, and I perceive that a little more clearly now that you have put it in somewhat different terms." In the latter case, the client's reaction is more like, "I am being diagnosed."

Thus, the crucial difference between counseling that is diagnostic and counseling based on empathic understanding is not in the words employed, but in the counselor's attitude. In effect, Rogers' criticism of diagnosis in counseling is directed against the diagnostic *attitude* of the counselor. This attitude places the counselor outside the frame of reference of the counselee. If it is present, the counselor will not communicate empathic understanding regardless of the words employed. "You resent her criticism" may succeed very well in capturing the essence of the counselee's feelings about her mother, but if this statement reflects a diagnostic attitude toward the counselee, this attitude and not the counselor's capacity to capture the essence of the counselee's feelings will be communicated. Whenever it occurs in counseling, the diagnostic attitude has a negative effect that no amount of technical skill can overcome.

But might Rogers' criticism of this diagnostic attitude make a new understanding of diagnosis possible? Since it is primarily this attitude that is inimical to effective counseling, is it possible to think of diagnosis apart from the diagnostic attitude itself?

Rogers alludes to this possibility in discussing diagnostic methods in other types of psychotherapy.[29] In the course of this discussion, he points out:

> Therapy is basically the experiencing of the inadequacies in old ways of perceiving, the experiencing of new and more accurate and adequate perceptions, and the recognition of significant relationships between perceptions. In a very meaningful and accurate sense, therapy *is* diagnosis, and this diagnosis is a process

which goes on in the experience of the client, rather than in the intellect of the clinician. It is in this way that the client-centered therapist has confidence in the efficacy of diagnosis. One might say that psychotherapy, of whatever orientation, is complete or almost complete when the diagnosis of the dynamics is experienced and accepted by the client. In client-centered therapy one could say that the purpose of the therapist is to provide the conditions in which the client is able to make, to experience, and to accept the diagnosis of the psychogenic aspects of his maladjustment.

Rogers concludes that client-centered therapy differs from other psychotherapeutic theories in that it does not build on "an externally based diagnosis." His point, therefore, is not that client-centered therapy lacks a diagnostic element, but that the diagnosis is not external to the process which goes on in the experience of the client. Experiencing the inadequacies of old ways of perceiving, experiencing new and more accurate ways of perceiving, and recognizing significant relationships between perceptions is itself diagnosis. But it is diagnosis internal to the counselee's own experience, not diagnosis initiated from an external diagnostic perspective.

This does not mean that the counselor is excluded from the diagnostic process. As Rogers points out, the therapist provides the conditions in which the client is able to make, experience, and accept the diagnosis. The therapist provides these conditions by relating to the counselee with empathic understanding, entering into the counselee's internal frame of reference. Thus, the counselor's empathic understanding provides the conditions for a more incisive diagnosis than is possible when diagnosis is a function of the diagnostic attitude. It makes possible a more accurate diagnostic process of perceiving and discriminating one's experiences.

A good illustration of how the empathic understanding of the counselor makes such diagnosis possible is the case of Mrs. Oak in Rogers' *On Becoming a Person.* [30] In this excerpt, the client is attempting to describe her experience of therapy. I quote it at some length so that the reader can see how diagnosis is a process of perceiving and discriminating one's experiences:

Client: It all comes pretty vague. But you know I keep, keep having the thought occur to me that this whole process for me is kind of like examining pieces of a jig-saw puzzle. It seems to me I, I'm in the process now of examining the individual pieces which really don't have too much meaning. Probably handling them, not even beginning to think of a pattern. . . . I pick up little pieces with absolutely no meaning except I mean the, the feeling that you get from simply handling them without seeing them as a pattern, but just from the touch, I probably feel, well it is going to fit someplace here.

Therapist: And that at the moment that, that's the process, just getting the feel and the shape and the configuration of the different pieces with a little bit of background feeling of, yeah they'll probably fit somewhere, but most of the attention's focused right on, "What does this feel like? And what's its texture?"

Client: That's right. There's almost something physical in it. A, a—

Therapist: You can't quite describe it without using your hands. A real, almost a sensuous sense in—

Client: That's right. Again it's, it's a feeling of being very objective, and yet I've never been quite so close to myself.

Therapist: Almost at one and the same time standing off and looking at yourself and yet somehow being closer to yourself that way than—

Throughout this excerpt, client and counselor engage in a process of discriminations. The client begins by saying that what she is experiencing in therapy remains conceptually vague, but that it is something like examining the pieces of a jigsaw puzzle and not yet knowing how they fit together. The therapist expresses his understanding of her efforts to clarify the experience of therapy when he says that, while she anticipates that the pieces of the puzzle will fit together somehow, at the present moment she is focusing most of her attention on the experience of examining each individual piece. Thus, he differentiates what is more in the forefront of her feelings from what is more in the background. He also communicates his understanding of the experience of examining each individual piece of the puzzle. It is something like examining not only the shape and configuration of the pieces but also their texture. She immediately agrees with this distinction between the shape and the texture of each piece of the puzzle, noting that there is something almost physical in it. If shape and configuration involve *visual* perception, exploring the texture of the experience involves getting the *feel* of it. In response, he observes that she communicates this sense of its tactile quality by using her hands to describe it. And this, in turn, leads to her observation that the experience feels both very objective and, at the same time, very close and personal. The therapist communicates his understanding of this paradoxical feeling by suggesting that in standing off and looking at herself she is also in that very process in closer contact with herself.

This excerpt from one of Rogers' counseling cases illustrates how the empathic understanding of the counselor makes possible a diagnostic process of discrimination. An aspect of Mrs. Oak's experience is described as being "not that, but this." Another feeling or perception is "both this and this." Still another feeling is "almost like that, but not quite." Throughout the excerpt, discriminations of an extremely subtle nature are being proposed and examined. Through empathic understanding, the counselor is able to recognize the subtle differences in the counselee's feelings and perceptions. She responds to many of his comments with a "that's right" and uses his observations as the springboard toward further discriminations. A diagnostic attitude would have been reflected in his inability to understand the subtle distinctions she wants to make. Moreover, in contrast to counseling based on the diagnostic attitude, the counselee is involved in the process. It was Mrs. Oak who made the first discrimination when she observed that there is a difference between examining the individual pieces of the puzzle and attempting to see how they fit together into an overall pattern. Thus, when diagnosis in counseling is fundamentally a matter of making more precise discriminations in one's experience, the counselee is at least as involved in diagnostic activity as the counselor.

This case also indicates that the diagnostic process can improve during the course of counseling. In this brief segment of a counseling session, there was a movement toward increasingly precise discriminations of the experience in question. This was possible not only because the counselor related to the counselee with empathic understanding, but also because the counselee took a more empathic view toward her own experience. Prior to undergoing counseling, the counselee is likely to take a *diagnostic attitude* toward these experiences, and this very attitude increases the difficulty of becoming more diagnostically acute. But through counseling, the tendency of counselees to take a diagnostic attitude toward their experiences—to view them from an external frame of reference—tends to give way to a more empathic understanding of these experiences, with the result that they are better able to make the penetrating kinds of discriminations reflected in this particular case.

A good illustration of how the *counselee* moves from the diagnostic attitude toward more empathic understanding is seen in another case in Rogers' *On Becoming a Person.* [31] The client is a young professional man who experiences physical tiredness after supper:

Client: It feels to me that in the past I used to fight a certain tiredness that I felt after supper. Well, now I feel pretty sure that I really *am tired—*

that I am not making myself tired—that I am just physiologically lower. It seemed that I was just constantly criticizing my tiredness.

Therapist: So you can let yourself *be* tired, instead of feeling along with it a kind of criticism of it.

Client: Yes, that I shouldn't be tired or something. And it seems in a way to be pretty profound that I can just not fight this tiredness, and along with it goes a real feeling of I've got to slow down, too, so that being tired isn't such an awful thing. I think I can also kind of pick up a thread here of why I should be that way in the way my father is and the way he looks at some of these things. For instance, say that I was sick, and I would report this, and it would seem that overtly he would want to do something about it but he would also communicate, "Oh, my gosh, more trouble." You know, something like that.

Therapist: As though there were something quite annoying really about being physically ill.

Client: Yeah, I'm sure that my father has the same disrespect for his own physiology that I have had. Now last summer I twisted my back, I wrenched it, I heard it snap and everything. There was real pain there all the time at first, real sharp. And I had the doctor look at it and he said it wasn't serious, it should heal by itself as long as I didn't bend too much. Well this was months ago—and I have been noticing recently that—hell, this is a real pain and it's still there —and it's not my fault.

Therapist: It doesn't prove something bad about you—

Client: No—and one of the reasons I seem to get more tired than I should maybe is because of this constant strain, and so—I have already made an appointment with one of the doctors at the hospital that he would look at it and take an X ray or something. In a way I guess you could say that I am just more accurately sensitive—or objectively sensitive to this kind of thing. . . .

In this case, the client's original tendency was to view his tiredness from a diagnostic attitude. He stood outside the experience and criticized it. Now, however, he views this experience of tiredness from a more internal frame of reference and thus understands it better. As he puts it, "I guess you could say that I am just more accurately sensitive—or objectively sensitive to this kind of thing." Moreover, with his increased understanding of the experience of tiredness, he no longer merely criticizes it but is taking concrete steps to do something about it. Thus, with increased discrimination of the experience comes a more accurate sense of what he can do to alleviate the problem. His empathic understanding of the experience is helping him devise a plan to resolve the problem. We have a tendency to view our own experiences from the external frame of the diagnostic attitude. But in this case, the counselee begins to discern that the experience of tiredness is not something he is making happen—and, therefore, something he needs to overcome—but is instead a "real" tiredness that reflects some underlying cause, possibly his earlier back injury. Thus, he moves from an external to an internal frame of reference and makes a more perceptive diagnosis of his experience of fatigue.

This analysis of Rogers' critique of the diagnostic attitude and argument for an internal diagnostic process invites two concluding comments. First, some might doubt the value of keeping "diagnosis" in our counseling vocabulary. It might be argued that there are other words for describing the kinds of discriminations that empathic understanding makes possible. Why retain the term "diagnosis" when it seems to imply the diagnostic attitude, thus inviting unnecessary misunderstanding? While these contentions have some merit, the word "diagnosis" should not be relinquished. As a consequence of client-centered therapy's critique of the diagnostic attitude, it is now possible to ascribe to "diagnosis" a meaning that has particular value in *pastoral* counseling.

For example, Paul W. Pruyser has recommended the recovery of the more traditional religious understanding of the word "diagnosis."[32] He points out:

> Although the words "diagnose" and "to diagnose" seem to have been all but absorbed by medicine, it will surprise no student of Greek to hear that they are general terms. They are used to mean discerning and discriminating in any field of knowledge, distinguishing one condition from another, and, by derivation, resolving or deciding. *Diagignoskein* ("distinguish") is differentiated on the one hand from *dokein* ("seem good," "think"), which leads to opinions and eventually dogmas, and on the other hand from *aisthanesthai* ("apprehend by the senses"), which means to perceive or view close to the level of appearance. To diagnose means grasping things as they really are, so as to do the right thing.

It is fair to say that the young professional man in the case described above replaced his earlier tendency to view his physical tiredness from the perspective of opinion *(dokein)* and appearance *(aisthanesthai)* and began to view it as it really was so as to do the right thing about it *(diagignoskein)*.

When diagnosis involves making accurate discriminations in order to do the right thing, it becomes an essential aspect of pastoral work. The pastor's job is to make distinctions and act on these distinctions:

> Thus regarded, diagnosis is very much a pastoral task also. It should be a substantial part of any pastor's activities. Who would deny that pastors need to approach their charges with a discerning knowledge of their condition, their situation, or their plight, and with discriminate ideas about desirable aid or interventions?

Thus, it might be possible to call the discriminating function of pastoral counseling by another name, thereby avoiding any suggestion that we have the diagnostic *attitude* in mind. However, the term "diagnosis" reflects a long-standing and very central purpose of the Christian ministry. It draws attention to the task of making accurate discriminations and acting responsibly on them. Thus, instead of relinquishing the term because of possible misunderstanding, we have chosen to preserve it by using Rogers' own discrimination between an external diagnostic attitude and an internal diagnostic process.

Our second comment concerning Rogers' discussion of diagnosis is that it focuses mainly on the *relationship* in counseling. The real issue is not what the counselor says to the counselee, but how one relates to the counselee. When the counselor relates to the counselee from an external frame of reference, a diagnostic attitude will inevitably result. But when the counselor relates to the counselee from an internal frame of reference, the diagnostic features of the counseling session will reflect empathic understanding. Moreover, diagnosis reflective of empathic understanding is based on the counselee's experience, not on the counselor's expertise and knowledge. As this experience is shared within the relationship itself, counselee and counselor participate together in discriminating the various features, dimensions, and meanings of this experience. Thus, the key to diagnosis is the relationship between counselee and counselor. Without an understanding relationship, the therapy will lack "the conditions in which the client is able to make, to experience, and to accept the diagnosis of the psychogenic aspects of his maladjustment."

This emphasis on the relationship between counselor and counselee in the diagnostic process has particular relevance for the integration of preaching and pastoral counseling. If empathic understanding leads to a more discriminating diagnostic process in counseling, this same type of relationship should prove equally valuable in the context of preaching. If replacement of the diagnostic attitude is important for pastoral counseling, it should be equally desirable that the preacher relinquish the external diagnostic attitude and enter the listeners' internal frame of reference. The diagnostic interpretation in the sermon should then reflect this internal perspective. But, one might object, is it not the case that the preacher, as one who speaks for God, needs to stand over against the congregation? Doesn't one's responsibility to speak for God require the external diagnostic attitude? This objection cannot be taken lightly. In fact, this same objection can be raised with regard to pastoral counseling. Is it not the case that the pastoral counselor is also a spokesman for God and therefore needs to stand over against the counselee and bring God's word to bear on the counselee's experiences? This objection requires us to focus on the diagnostic uses of theology in pastoral counseling. As one who speaks for God, the pastoral counselor has a theological task. Problems may be diagnosed psychologically, but they must be diagnosed theologically. The question, then, is whether theological understandings can be used diagnostically within a framework of empathic understanding? Or does the diagnostic use of theological understandings require the external diagnostic attitude? Put another way, does the pastoral counselor relinquish the perspective of empathic understanding when diagnosing the counselee's experiences in theological terms? The answer to this question has direct implications for preaching.

The Diagnostic Role of Theology in Pastoral Counseling

How can theology be used diagnostically in the counseling session without requiring the counselor to adopt an external frame of reference? While Pruyser does not address this question directly, his discussion of the diagnostic uses of theology in pastoral counseling helps clarify it. In viewing theology as a diagnostic instrument in pastoral counseling, Pruyser is aware that theology was considered a diagnostic instrument long before modern psychotherapy came on the scene. He notes that "theological-diagnostic" literature has always had a central place in Christian spirituality. For example, in speaking about "distinguishing marks" of saintliness and the "qualifications of those that are in favor with God and entitled to his eternal rewards," Jonathan Edwards proved himself to be "a penetrating diagnostician who went well beyond surface impressions. He distinguished between good and poor diagnostic indicators and felt that some 'signs' are suspect, if not worthless." Pruyser acknowledges that Edwards' diagnostic approach tends at times to be quite paternalistic, thus reflective of the "diagnostic attitude" discussed above. But Edwards also stresses the importance of including the individual believer in the diagnostic process. Pruyser asks, "How many doctors today have shed the paternalistic heritage to the extent that they would allow the diagnostic process to be a truly participatory enterprise on the part of the patient?" In comparison with much medical practice today, Edwards' approach to diagnosis reflected greater empathic understanding.

Søren Kierkegaard's work is also reflective of the diagnostic uses of theology. For him, the task is "self-diagnosis." Thus, to a greater extent than Edwards,

> the trained theologian and his charge are in this case one and the same person. He artfully conducts an intrapsychic dialogue concealed by introducing two fictitious parties arguing with each other. Kierkegaard does not introduce a diagnostic system, and there is little in his writings that will strike us as pastoral. Nevertheless, his work contains much that can be seen as a demonstration of self-diagnosing within an exquisitely theological framework.

While it might appear that Kierkegaard's project of self-diagnosis was narcissistic, this project actually supports Rogers' principle that the most personal is also the most general. Self-diagnosis that is done within a "theological framework" is the direct opposite of narcissism.

We may also include William James's *The Varieties of Religious Experience* in the company of theological-diagnostic literature.[33] Though James does not claim to be a theologian, he shares Edwards' concern to discriminate between types and quality of religious "affections." James differentiates "sick-minded" and "healthy-minded" forms of religiosity, compares the quality and effects of sudden and gradual conversions, and discriminates various forms of religious saintliness. This is essentially a diagnostic enterprise, one which is conducted from an internal frame of reference. James is not the external observer, taking a perspective outside the frame of reference of the believer. Unlike the diagnostic attitude that would claim that believers are unaware of the "real" meaning of their religious thoughts and behavior, James attempts to empathically understand believers' own accounts of their religious experiences. Thus, his contribution to theological diagnosis is in not placing the religious experiences within an externally derived philosophical or psychological schema, but in identifying the subtle discriminations that are already present in individuals' own accounts of their religious experience. If Edwards' diagnosis of such experiences leans somewhat toward the diagnostic attitude, James's approach is more reflective of the internal diagnostic process.

Finally, Pruyser offers his own approach to theological diagnosis. He recommends using certain rather familiar theological concepts (providence, faith, grace, repentance, awareness of the holy, vocation, and communion) as "guideposts" for use in diagnosing the counselee's problem. One of the counseling cases in Pruyser's book shows how these "guideposts" can be faithful to the internal frame of reference of the counselee. For example, Lambert was a college student who had been rejected by his girl friend. In reconstructing the problem, he indicated that he now felt guilty for having engaged in sexual acts with the young woman. As the counseling process moved from the reconstruction to the more explicitly diagnostic stage, the pastor communicated his impressions to the young man. He noted his counselee's desire to repent of past sins, and assured him of "God's loving providential care for the whole of his life." This assurance struck home to the young man, because he "picked this up by dwelling on the positive elements of his friendship with the girl, as if to contrast his feeling of uncleanliness with feelings of gratitude."

As far as we can judge, the pastor succeeded in assuming the internal frame of reference of the counselee. While the counselee might not have chosen words like "providence" and "repentance" to describe his perception of the experience, these terms did discriminate between the various feelings he was having. The use of the term "providence" is not intrinsically different from Rogers' case where the counselor commented on his counselee's desire to gain a sense of the "texture" of her experiences. "Texture" may not be the word she would have chosen to communicate her experience, but she quickly accepted the term as accurate. In the same way, the college student quickly responded to the pastor's use of the term "providence," demonstrating its accuracy by focusing on the positive aspects of his relationship to his girl friend.

Thus, the use of theological language in counseling is not necessarily a lapse into the diagnostic attitude. When sensitively employed, these theological themes can communicate an empathic understanding of the counselee's experience. The use of theological themes for diagnostic purposes does not necessarily place the counselor in an external frame of reference. In fact, these themes may actually help the counselor enter into the counselee's internal frame of reference. Since many pastors today are likely to be more confident about their knowledge of psychotherapeutic theories than about their competence in theology, it may be that greater attention to the diagnostic uses of theological themes will enable them to relinquish their sense of superior knowledge and expertise acquired from familiarity with psychotherapeutic theories, and thereby to shift from an external to an internal frame of reference. One's very lack of confidence regarding theological concepts may enable one to enter into the counselee's experience as a fellow explorer rather than as the diagnostic expert. If so, an attitudinal shift from psychotherapist to practical theologian need not mean exchanging one external frame of reference for another. It can in fact prove the key to entry into the counselee's internal frame of reference.

The Guilt-Ridden Parishioner

Let us conclude our exploration of the diagnostic use of theology in pastoral counseling by assessing an excerpt from a counseling case reported in Cryer and Vayhinger's *Casebook in Pastoral Counseling*.[34] This case enables us to see how the use of theology in a diagnostic way would have enabled the counselor to enter the counselee's internal frame of reference.

The counselee, John, had called the pastor earlier in the week and asked for an appointment to talk. When he comes in, he tells the pastor that things are pretty mixed up in his whole life, and that he thinks he knows the reason for this, but can't seem to figure it out. Then, quite abruptly, he has a question, and there is this exchange:

John: Reverend, can God forgive people?
Pastor: I think he can. What do you think about it?
John: I don't know. I thought so too, but that was before. Now I don't know—I don't know.
Pastor: You have some doubts about the forgiving nature of God?

Stage 2: Reconstruction of the Problem

John: Yeah—maybe I better tell you. It was five years ago. I've never told anybody this. It's been bothering me so much I just had to tell somebody: I killed five men. It was during the Korean War. I just got married and was drafted and went overseas right away. One night when we were out on patrol, three of us and the lieutenant went out on a mission. I was the only one who came back. We started out and everything was okay. We got there and took care of our mission and on the way back it happened—we were ambushed. I sort of got cut off from the others. I heard shots. I laid in the grass. They went on by; then I found myself behind the lines and couldn't get back. I wasn't too sure where I was so I just started crawling. Then I saw them: three pillboxes on one side and a river on the other. The only way I could get them was one at a time. So I did. Crawled up—Couldn't shoot—too many —pulled out my knife, bayonet, got all five, one at a time. Didn't bother me much at first, even when I came back from the war. Didn't bother too much. But then I got to thinking about it. All the time God says, "Thou shalt not kill." But I did. I killed —five of them—stuck a knife right through each one.

Pastor: This has caused you some amount of worry since you have come back?

John: Yeah. You know how I've been with the church. I started sort of worrying more and more all the time. God is supposed to be able to forgive people, but this is sort of different. This isn't the same thing as when you preach up there on Sunday morning. You sort of get up and tell about these people. The little things—cheating at business, a heavy finger on the scale, or something like that—but this is different. This is a big business; this is murder.

Pastor: The experience in the army is a very big thing to you in relation to some of the things we preach about?

John: Not so much the experience, but the killing. I just killed these men. I know, it might have been them or me. Maybe it would have been better if it had been me. I don't know. I've just been waiting, waiting for something to happen. I don't think God can just come out and forgive this kind of thing. I don't know. Just seems—I don't know.

Pastor: Things have been building up inside of you, and you have begun to question God's activity in this?

John: Yeah, I guess, sort of. Well, God—he's running the universe you might say. You just can't go around killing people right and left without being punished for it. God just doesn't sit there and let you stab people and let you get away with it. In our society, just like a man kills somebody, we kill him sometimes. This is almost the same thing. I mean, you take a life. You just don't go out and do this. You say, "Well, it's over with, it's part of the war"; but it's more than that. It's a man you killed. Just like if I killed somebody now, it's the same thing.

Pastor: Then you are wondering now how God can forgive one who has killed?

John: Yeah, that's about it. I don't know. I've been waiting; I've been hoping; I've even been praying. But I don't think he's forgiven me. He—I just keep worrying. Now I think I'm going to get punished; I don't know. I know he's going to punish me somehow. I don't know how. But I think this is it; this is what's bothering me. I just keep waiting, looking every day. I wake up and I look out and I think, well, maybe today he'll punish me so I can go on living like I should. But he hasn't punished me. He just keeps me waiting.

Pastor: Waiting for punishment is a terrible threat.

John: Yes. You just don't kill somebody and get away with it. I mean, it's different; it's not like these little things. It is vital, vital to people. They got to live.

Pastor: In other words, killing is a rather large issue in the world today. More so than some of the other things, some of the smaller things you feel we talk about. This would make a very large problem; this would make one worry.

John: Well, killing is taking away life.

Pastor: Life seems important to you?

John: Yeah, I guess so. You can't live without life. Without life, what is there? I mean, I live; I got life. Why shouldn't the next guy have life? Why shouldn't he live the same way. You know—but I, I don't know. When you do something wrong, you have to pay. You just can't forget about it, cast it off, and don't worry about it. You have to pay, God makes everyone pay.

Pastor: You feel that somehow God must have punishment for the wrong deeds of man?

John: Yeah. I know—I know we preach love all the time. Everybody says all we need is love. God forgives, loves everybody, everything is going to be okay. This is okay. But even with this love, sure, sure God loves us. He loves, he wants us, and everything; but you can't get away with this. There are certain laws, like the Ten Commandments. When you break them, sure he still loves you, but even then you still have to pay for these bad deeds which you do.

Pastor: The idea of love and hate, then, is a problem with you in relation to God?

John: God doesn't hate necessarily. But there are certain things when you do something wrong you have to pay for it.

Pastor: Punishment rather than hate?

John: Yeah. . . .

John's agonized portrayal of his killings and their continuing effect on his life could be diagnosed in terms of Pruyser's theological themes. There is the primary theme of *repentance:* "I have said that I am sorry and willing to take my punishment, but the punishment never comes." There is the subordinate theme of *providence:* "My future is bleak, not so much because of the fear that God is planning to punish me but because he keeps delaying the punishment that is rightfully mine." Conspicuous by its absence is the theme of *grace:* "The most loving thing that God could do would be to punish me and get this awful waiting over with."

In addition to these implicit theological themes, found woven into the narrative, John makes a number of explicit theological and ethical judgments. For example: (1) Killing is not like cheating at business; it is much more serious. (That is, there are different levels of sin.) (2) Killing is killing regardless of whether it occurs in war or under normal social conditions. (That is, killing is not a contextual matter.) (3) God has to punish me. Some wrongs do not require punishment, but if there is anything that requires punishment, killing certainly does. (4) God punishes even while he loves us. In fact, he could show his love by getting the punishment over with. (5) Punishment is inevitable. It has nothing to do with God hating me. He simply has no other choice than to punish me. But he is making me wait for it.

Generally speaking, the counselor fails to enter into John's internal frame of reference as John raises these theological and moral issues. He appears reluctant to participate in John's efforts to sort out his feelings about God, sin, and punishment. Empathic understanding in this case would require entering into the counselee's efforts to diagnose his problem theologically. Is there no difference between killing in war and killing under normal social conditions? Does God have to punish the counselee for his crimes? If so, what would constitute appropriate punishment? Might his guilty conscience be punishment enough? Can his own suffering, no matter how severe, ever atone for the deaths of five men? Are religious concepts being used here to support a legalistic understanding of his relation to God, when his war experiences are forcing on him a more complex understanding of that relationship?

These are just a few of the many theological and moral issues that are involved in the counselee's effort to diagnose his problem. The counselor could have entered into these theological issues in a more empathically understanding way. He is not very comfortable with these theological notions, however, and responds to John's theological diagnoses in a questioning tone, as though John's ideas about God and punishment have a strange and foreign quality to them, rather than entering into these reflections of John's with real understanding. He also, at times, attempts to replace theological with psychological language. He suggests that John is worried, feelings are building up inside, he feels threatened, anxious, and so forth. While occasionally accurate, this psychological language reflects a diagnostic attitude, whereas responding to the counselee's efforts to understand his experience theologically would have meant entering into his internal frame of reference.

Ironically, this failure to enter into John's internal frame of reference also causes the pastor to miss some important *psychological* dynamics. Often, his psychological language misses the emotional level of John's account. After John gives his recital of his killings, the pastor says, "This has caused you some amount of worry since you have come back." Or when John says, "Well, killing is taking away life," the pastor responds with, "Life seems important to you?" Had he really entered into these theological discriminations with John, the pastor would have gotten much more deeply into the intensity of John's struggle with his guilt, his profound longing for punishment, and his deep desire to be rid of the burden of guilt. He would also have recognized that John's act of violence against the soldiers—so cool, so efficient, yet so horrible—challenged his self-perception as a man who was good, not given to aggressive or vengeful behavior. Thus, instead of obscuring the psychological dynamics in this case, attention to the task of theological diagnosis would actually have helped to clarify them. Not only that, theological diagnosis would have revealed John's hope that somehow his positive self-image could be restored.

Conclusion

Perhaps it can be argued that the above case is unique. Is it characteristic of individuals who seek pastoral counseling to want to explore their relationship to God? In fact, is it not true that most individuals would resent the pastor's efforts to introduce theological considerations into the counseling session? Two comments on this. First, Pruyser's case of Lambert indicates that theological concerns can be *implicit* in what a counselee says; in such cases, using theological themes diagnostically means entering into the tacit level of the counselee's internal frame of reference. Thus, just because the counselee does not use religious language does not mean that theological diagnosis in such a case would necessarily reflect a diagnostic attitude. Second, while there is always the danger that a counselor's use of theology will reflect the diagnostic attitude, there is also the danger that a counselor will take a diagnostic attitude toward the counselee's desire to explore his experiences in a theologically diagnostic way. The casebook from which the case of John was taken is indicative of the high proportion of counseling sessions that involve theological diagnoses formulated not by the pastor but by the counselee. There is the eighty-nine-year-old woman who continues to pray but feels that God is awfully far away at times, the middle-aged woman whose physical illness has resulted in a "loss of faith," and the middle-aged man who wants to talk to the pastor about the fact that he is not "living right." In all three cases, the pastor failed to enter into the counselee's internal frame of reference by declining to participate in the theological diagnosis which the counselee initiated. The theological concerns raised by the parishioner are typically judged by the pastor (in his postmortem comments on the session) to be important aspects of the counseling session; but the pastor usually congratulates himself for resisting the impulse, as one pastor put it, "to respond to his religious problems with intellectual answers."

In making a case for the positive uses of theology as a diagnostic tool in pastoral counseling, I am mindful that there is at present little emphasis on diagnosis in the counseling theories used in pastoral counseling. Pruyser's book is exceptional in this regard. Thus, the question arises: Where are pastors to turn for guidance in their diagnostic use of theology in counseling? Where can they turn for resources? How can one gain experience in an other than trial-and-error fashion? In my judgment, the theological-diagnostic literature to which Pruyser alludes can be of only limited assistance to the pastor in this regard. While Edwards, Kierkegaard, and other "diagnostic theologians" may be helpful to some extent, it is difficult to translate their work into the specific resources needed in the pastoral counseling setting. The best source of guidance is the diagnostic use of theology in preaching. Pastors, by their own use of theological diagnosis in their preaching each Sunday, can gain invaluable experience toward developing an effective diagnostic approach in counseling. Also, one can learn how theology functions diagnostically by reading and analyzing published sermons. Chapter 4 illustrates how published sermons offer examples of theological diagnosis that can prove useful in pastoral counseling.

Chapter 4

Theological Diagnosis in Preaching

How does theology function diagnostically in preaching? Are there different *types* of theological diagnosis? If so, are they adaptable to the counseling setting?

In what follows I will identify six types of theological diagnosis in sermons. Then I will explore the potential uses of these types in pastoral counseling. In discussing the latter issue, we will consider which types are more likely to reflect the diagnostic attitude and which are more responsive to the internal frame of reference.

Types of Theological Diagnosis in Sermons

In focusing on these six types, I make no claim to completeness. There are probably as many types of theological diagnosis as there are preachers. On the other hand, individual preachers tend to adopt a certain type of theological diagnosis and stay with it. They generally do not move from one type of theological diagnosis to another. The specific problem being addressed on a given Sunday does not dictate the type of theological diagnosis used in that sermon. Hence, theological diagnosis provides continuity from sermon to sermon. It becomes the major identifying feature of a preacher's sermons. Moreover, while it is often difficult to determine how the formal theological position of a given preacher (conservative, orthodox, neo-orthodox, liberal) shapes his or her sermons, it is not very difficult to discern the influence of a preacher's preferred mode of theological diagnosis.

In our discussion of the six types, sermons of a single preacher will be used to illustrate each type. We will focus in every case on the diagnostic interpretation stage of the sermons.

1. *Theological diagnosis that identifies underlying personal motivations.* This type of theological diagnosis is concerned to expose the personal motives that are responsible for the problem. Identifying these motives is considered the way to penetrate to the heart of the problem and begin dealing with the problem more effectively. Identifying these motives is difficult, however, because we are largely unaware of them. The preacher anticipates that listeners will be surprised, even resistant, to the suggestion that a certain motive is involved in the problem. Moreover, he may feel that they would prefer a more superficial explanation. It is especially difficult to accept the claim that the problem is due to some defect in one's own motivational structure. It is easier to believe that it is due to social conditions, or to some other cause that shifts responsibility away from oneself.

John Henry Newman's sermons are excellent examples of this type of theological diagnosis.[35] "Love, the One Thing Needful," which we discussed in Chapter 2, exposes the personal motives responsible for the instability of our religious faith. He suggests that the underlying problem is motivational; we are *deficient in love.* Why do we find it so difficult genuinely to repent of our sins? Why are we so open to the power of excitement and novelty in religious life? Why is our Christian faith so inadequate in times of affliction? These and other signs of the instability of our faith are due to the fact that

> we are deficient in love. He who loves cares little for anything else. The world may go as it will; he sees and hears it not, for his thoughts are drawn another way; he is solicitous mainly to walk with God, and to be found with God; and is in perfect peace because he is stayed in him.

Newman's diagnosis centers on the fact that, if we were motivated by the love of God, the problems that upset our faith would no longer do so. But we are deficient in this positive motive and, as a result, negative motives gain the upper hand.

In "Hollow Obedience," Newman is again exposing defective personal motives. This sermon, based on the Old Testament story of Balaam (Numbers 22), points out that Balaam is typical of individuals whose seemingly right actions are based on wrong motives. Balaam's motivational "defect lay in this, that he had not a single eye towards God's will, but was ruled by other objects." Evidence of this defect is the fact that Balaam exaggerated his desire to be obedient to God's will:

> And here we see why he spoke so much and so vauntingly of his determination to follow God's direction. He made a great *point* of following it; his end was not to please God, but to keep straight with him. He who loves does not act from calculation or reasoning; he does not in his cool moments reflect upon or talk of what he is doing, as if it were a great sacrifice. Much less does he pride himself on it; but this is what Balaam seems to have done.

Balaam's motives are diagnosed as defective because his obedience is too calculated, too carefully rationalized. His own explanation of his actions reveals that his underlying motivation is not to follow the will of God in singleminded fashion. Rather, he is motivated by a variety of self-seeking interests.

In "The Weapons of Saints," Newman indicates why the exposure of defective motives is so important to the Christian life. He acknowledges that "no one is safe from the intrusion of corrupt motives," and he warns of the danger of "allowing" wrong motives to become the driving force of one's life. We need continual reminders of the destructive effects of corrupt motives that can so control our lives that we no longer realize our motives are defective. The preacher's diagnostic task, therefore, is to continue to expose the motives that underlie our actions, recognizing that listeners may resist this exposure because they have developed an elaborate defense against it. Newman meets this potential resistance by pointing out to his listeners that his diagnosis may not seem persuasive at first glance, but it becomes more and more compelling as we allow it to penetrate our defenses. Thus, in "Love, the One Thing Needful," Newman prefaces his diagnosis with the comment, "I must say plainly this, that, fanciful though it may appear at first sight to say so . . ." And in "The Weapons of Saints" he prefaces his diagnosis with the statement, "It is strange to say, but it is a truth which our own observation and experience will confirm . . ." With such comments, Newman prepares his listeners to hear the "truth" about themselves and to begin the process of purifying their motives.

2. *Theological diagnosis that identifies the range of potential causes.* The first type of theological diagnosis attempts to uncover the *single* motive that is at the root of the problem. This second type explores the whole range of personal and situational factors that might cause this particular problem to emerge. The preacher offers a veritable checklist from which listeners may select the most likely cause of their own particular difficulties with the problem.

John Wesley's sermons are an excellent example of this second type of theological diagnosis.[36] For example, in "Heaviness Through Manifold Temptations," Wesley provides an extensive list of the possible reasons why an individual, once content in the faith, might become disheartened and discouraged. Possible causes of this "heaviness of soul" are bodily diseases, nervous disorders, financial poverty, bereavement, the apostasy of loved ones and friends, knowledge of our inner corruption, and God's withdrawal from our presence. In assessing these possible causes, Wesley is most concerned with the latter two. He stresses the fact that knowledge of our sins need not lead us to become disheartened, because God will increase the knowledge of his love in direct proportion to increases in our knowledge of our inner corruption. He also notes that the sense of *God's withdrawal* has been emphasized by mystics, who may well be misconstruing God's methods of drawing individuals to himself as absolute withdrawal. If God appears to have left us, this most likely means that he wants us to follow where he has gone. Wesley provides a significant number of possible causes for the condition of "heaviness of soul" and invites his listeners to apply this list to their own situations. He does not impose a single causal explanation for this condition, nor does he suggest that the cause is necessarily a personal deficiency. It can also be a situational factor, such as bereavement, that is largely beyond one's control.

In "The Wilderness State," Wesley takes up a related problem, the feeling of being in a spiritual wilderness—"a waste and howling desert"—where the usual evidences of God's trust and love are strangely absent. His diagnosis again focuses on a range of potential causes which he places in three general categories: (1) sin, anger, or taking offense, and inordinate desire and carelessness; (2) ignorance of the Scriptures and of the way God works in the soul; and (3) temptation. In citing these three types of causes of the experience of being spiritually lost, Wesley emphasizes that the will of God is clearly not among them. God never desires that we experience his desertion, and he never repents of having given us his gifts.

Thus, in cataloging the possible causes of any given problem, Wesley regularly discriminates between causes that might be involved and causes that are definitely ruled out. In general, causes that are ruled out are those which suggest that God either is the perpetrator of the problem or wants us to have it. This ascription of liability to God is consistently resisted. Rather, one is to look for causes from among known personal and situational factors. The preacher's task is to help listeners identify the cause from the range of potential causes, and to caution against including causes that would ascribe negative intentions to God.

3. *Theological diagnosis that exposes inadequate formulations of the problem.* This third type of theological diagnosis

exposes inaccurate formulations of the problem in order to clear the way for a deeper understanding of it. While the two preceding types emphasized the basic *causes* of the problem, this type pursues a deeper understanding of the problem itself. The preacher's diagnostic task is to encourage listeners to abandon superficial understandings and to risk opening themselves up to its deeper meanings. The reason this requires risk is that the deeper meanings of the problem reveal the ambiguities of human existence. Once these deeper meanings have been exposed, it is more difficult to think in terms of "resolving" the problem. More likely one will need to learn to live with its inherent ambiguity.

Paul Tillich's sermons reflect this type of theological diagnosis.[37] For example, in "The Meaning of Providence," Tillich says that there are few articles of the Christian faith that have more importance for our daily lives than providence, but few are surrounded by so many misunderstandings. These misunderstandings have led many to be disillusioned with Christianity. Thus, the diagnostic task is to expose misunderstandings of providence in order to make way for a true understanding of it. First, providence is not a vague promise that, with the help of God, everything will come to a good end; there are many situations in life that come to a bad end. Second, it is not the maintenance of hope in every situation; some situations are hopeless. Third, it is not the anticipation of a period in history in which providence will be proved by human happiness and goodness; there will be no future generation in which divine providence will be any less paradoxical than it is in our own. Fourth, providence is not a divine plan that predetermines everything. Providence does not mean any of these things. Instead, it means

> that there is a creative and saving possibility implied in every situation, which cannot be destroyed by any event. Providence means that the daemonic and destructive forces within ourselves and our world can never have an unbreakable grasp upon us, and that the bond which connects us with the fulfilling love can never be disrupted.

Thus, providence means that there is nothing that can ultimately separate us from the love of God: *"This* is the faith in providence, and this alone." All other understandings of providence are rejected; only this one stands. And, most important, providence in this view is, at one and the same time, the most pervasive and the most difficult to concretize.

In "You Are Accepted," Tillich deals with the problem of God's acceptance of us. What does it mean to experience acceptance? In his view, the Christian understanding of *grace* is the key to the meaning of acceptance. But, if this is so, false understandings of grace need to be exposed in order to clear the way for the true meaning. In exposing these false understandings, Tillich observes:

> For some people, grace is the willingness of a divine king and father to forgive over and again the foolishness and weakness of his subjects and children. We must reject such a concept of grace; for it is a merely childish destruction of a human dignity. For others, grace is a magic power in the dark places of the soul, but a power without any significance for practical life, a quickly vanishing and useless idea. For others, grace is the benevolence that we may find beside the cruelty and destructiveness in life. But then, it does not matter whether we say "life goes on," or whether we say "there is grace in life"; if grace means no more than this, the word should, and will, disappear. For other people, grace indicates the gifts that one has received from nature or society, and the power to do good things with the help of those gifts.

If these understandings of grace are inadequate, then what is grace? Grace is "the *re*union of life with life, the *re*conciliation of the self with itself. Grace is the acceptance of that which is rejected." Unlike the other interpretations of grace, this understanding both encourages us to look "down into ourselves to discover there the struggle between separation and reunion, between sin and grace, in our relation to others, in our relation to ourselves, and in our relation to the Ground and aim of our being." Thus, it goes more deeply into our inner struggles, our sense of internal estrangement. Unless we view grace at this deeper level, we have not plumbed its full power, and we have therefore not understood its full meaning. On the other hand, this deeper understanding of grace is less likely to be thought of as a means of "resolving" the problem of acceptance. It is not a specific gift, it is not forgiveness of a specific act of foolishness or weakness, it is not a magic power. Rather, it is power we experience in our ongoing struggle to overcome separation and estrangement. Thus, when viewed as acceptance of what is rejected, grace is both more powerful and less easily concretized than the inadequate understandings suggest.

While Tillich is concerned to expose superficial understandings of the problem to which the sermon is addressed, he does not contend that his interpretation clears up all its mysteries. In fact, the interpretation chosen is persuasive precisely because it takes seriously the paradoxes of human existence. Thus, in "Knowledge Through Love" he points out: "Our very being is a continuous asking for the *meaning* of our being, a continuous attempt to decipher the enigma of our world and our heart." The interpretations that Tillich rejects, therefore, are formulations of the problem that evade the enigmatic character of human life. As he says of the apostle Paul:

> Paul experienced the breakdown of a system of life and thought which he believed to be a whole, a perfect truth without riddle or gaps. He then found himself buried under the pieces of his knowledge and his morals. But Paul never tried again to build up a new, comfortable house out of the pieces. He dwelt with the pieces. He realized always that fragments remain fragments, even if one attempts to reorganize them. The unity to which they belong lies beyond them; it is grasped through hope, but not face to face.

Paul was able to endure the fragmentary nature of knowledge, however, because the fragments themselves had acquired a new meaning for him. In like fashion, the deeper "answers" to problems are not more complete or final than those they replace. On the contrary, they leave us persuaded that our understanding of the problem is fragmentary. On the other hand, we are better able to endure this because we are also more conscious of the necessity of viewing problems in the light of the existence of a larger reality of "something beyond . . . riddles and enigmas."

4. *Theological diagnosis that draws attention to untapped personal and spiritual resources.* In this type of theological diagnosis, the preacher points out that our problems would seem more manageable if we would recognize our vast store of personal and spiritual resources. In failing to do this, we allow the problem to immobilize us. Thus, this form of theological diagnosis brings to our awareness the strengths and resources we possess but for one reason or another have failed to employ.

Phillips Brooks's sermons reflect this form of theological diagnosis.[38] In "Visions and Tasks," Brooks discusses the role that vision plays in inspiring persons to carry out difficult tasks. Individuals who reach middle adulthood tend to lose their enthusiasm for the tasks they are responsible to perform:

> A man we see sometimes who, as he comes to middle-life, finds his immediate enthusiastic sight of ideal things grown dull; that is the almost necessary condition of his ripening life. He does not spring as quickly as he once did to seize each newly offered hope for man. A thousand disenchantments have made him serious and sober. He looks back, and the glow and sparkle which he once saw in life he sees no longer. He wonders at his recollection of himself, and asks how it is possible that life ever should have seemed to him as he remembers that it did seem.

What can such a man do? What resources do persons like him already possess to bring them out of their dullness and disenchantment? The fact that they once had visions and dreams they now suspect to be illusions is the very resource they need to remain constant in their tasks. The fact that life once seemed bright and filled with possibility is now their "most valued certainty." A man therefore should

not part with that assurance for anything. All the hard work that
he does now is done in the strength and light of that remembered
enthusiasm. . . . Every day the dreams of his boyhood, which
seem dead, are really the live inspirations of his life.

Persons who are discouraged in middle life have the necessary resource to overcome this discouragement if they can
only recognize it. The preacher's diagnostic task is to direct
their attention to these resources.

In "The Egyptians Dead Upon the Seashore," Brooks
addresses the criticism that his continuing emphasis on the
resources available to cope with the problems of temptation
and sin is "the mere dream of an optimistic sermon." In
response, he appeals to his listeners to consult their own
experience and ask whether "God has not sometimes given
you the right to such a hope?" In looking back over the past,
have there not been some real victories in your life? For
example,

Are there not at least some temptations to which you yielded
then to which you know that you can never yield again? Are
there not some meannesses which you once thought glorious
which now you know are mean? Are there no places where you
once stumbled where now you know you can walk firm?

Brooks goes on to say, however, that he is not appealing
merely to experience but also to the Christian truth about
humanity. When Christ takes hold of the natural man,

no longer can that nature think itself doomed to evil. Intensely
sensitive to feel the presence of evil as he never felt it before, the
Christian man instantly and intensely knows that evil is a stran-
ger and an intruder in his life. The wonder is not that it should
some day be cast out: the wonder is that it should ever have come
in.

Thus, Brooks contends that his diagnosis of any given problem is not mere optimism, but is rooted in the conviction that
the Christian faith has real, practical power. Through Christ
there is victory over temptation and sin.

This type of theological diagnosis, therefore, emphasizes that the problem has not been adequately diagnosed until we have identified the available resources for dealing with it. While we are inclined to recognize only the strength and tenacity of the problem itself, theological diagnosis directs attention to the greater strength we possess for overcoming it. As long as a person looks only at his limitations, his self-knowledge and his understanding of God is seriously distorted: "How can he know what lurking power lies packed away within the near-opened folds of this inactive life? Has he ever dared to call himself the child of God, and for one moment felt what that involves?" Brooks concludes: "There is nothing on earth more seemingly significant and more absolutely insignificant than men's judgment of their own moral and spiritual limitations."

5. *Theological diagnosis that brings clarity to the problem.* The fifth type of diagnosis uses theology to gain as clear a picture of the problem as possible. It suggests that the reason we have difficulties with a particular problem is that we have not yet gotten it clarified. As long as the problem itself remains confused and befuddled, we will not be able to do much about it. Therefore, the preacher's task is to clarify the problem, to help listeners gain a clear understanding of what the problem is and what it entails. The assumption here is that problems lend themselves to clarification. While the third type recognizes that the problems with which the Christian faith is concerned are enigmatic and paradoxical, this type contends that the fundamental problems of Christian faith can be rendered clear and transparent. It is not that the problems themselves are enigmatic, but that we Christians leave these problems in a confused and unexamined state because, for one reason or another, we lack the interest or the will to clarify them.

A good representative of this type is Austin Farrer.[39] His sermon "In Season and Out," which we discussed in Chapter 2, seeks to clarify the problem of *variation in our religious lives* by suggesting that "we may get some light on the matter by observing the difference between steady marriages and exciting love affairs." This desire to "get some light on the matter" is characteristic of Farrer's theological diagnoses. In his sermon "The Witch of Endor," he takes up the issue of the appropriate Christian attitude toward modern spiritualists and psychics. He suggests that these spiritualists and psychics direct our attention away from those experiences in which God is clearly perceived to those experiences in which his presence is veiled and obscure. Thus,

> if God is a living will and a heart of love directly concerned for us, why should we look for him, or why listen for him, in the remote and dubious margins of our experience? It is folly, without a doubt, if we are looking for the evidence of God's creative work, to turn from the living panorama of nature and strain our eyes into the remotest origins of the universe, where we shall descry nothing but the emptiest of astronomical conjecture. And so it is folly, if we seek the master of our life, to look away from the point where God's will touches us in our present existence, into fields where perhaps, perhaps, the sensitive soul makes contact with a limbo beyond the reach or control of reasonable thought.

Here, the issue of spiritualism comes down to the matter of clarity. Why "strain our eyes" to see God when "God is here, and we can know him if we will make our account with him: if we will accept his forgiveness for us, and his love for our neighbors, and his plain will for our duty."

Farrer continues the same emphasis on clarity in his sermon "Moral Perfection Not Enough." Observing that university people abandon the Christian faith and become humanists because Christianity appears morally tepid and intellectually weak, Farrer points out that the Christian faith provides a moral and intellectual clarity that humanists fail to discern. The Christian faith is no less influenced by reason and moral conscience than humanism:

> The enlightened Christian goes by reason and by conscience, like the enlightened humanist. But for the Christian, "conscience" isn't my feeling about me, it's God's judgement of me, and

"reason" isn't my power to do moral sums, it's my power to see how the Creator has ordered his creation.

Farrer also points out that, while the humanist says Christianity is obscurantist and based on superstition, the Christian faith not only does not distort reality but is the one perspective that is not based on deception: "The divine light shines in unbelieving as well as in believing hearts, but believers have the happiness not to be deceived about its source." Thus, Christianity reflects a clear vision of human life. For Christians, "there is one heavenly truth, the common light of day, showing all things in their true colors."

In "Inspiration by the Spirit," Farrer explores the claim made by many Christians that a particular decision of theirs was "inspired" by God. He says that the trouble with such claims is that they smother reason. An individual who says that he did what the Spirit directed implies that this was the only reason he did what he did. But there are not fewer reasons for what God ordains but infinitely more. Thus, in place of a theory of inspiration that attributes all agency for one's actions to God, Farrer recommends cultivating a "spiritual perceptiveness" that is capable of gaining insight into the various reasons for one's actions. The individual who received an "inspiration" from God not to allow the surgeon to amputate her leg was responding, at least in part, to fear: "What hit cousin Harriet with the force of divine authority was something which came rushing up from the bottom of her mind, and I could put a name to it—so could you—it was animal fear, the fear of the surgeon's knife." Thus, in contrast to a view of divine inspiration in which one absolves oneself of responsibility for understanding one's actions, Farrer stresses the need for greater "intellectual sight" in the Christian faith.

Farrer's diagnostic method emphasizes the importance of clarity in dealing with any issue of religious faith. Christians have a primary responsibility to perceive their lives and those around them without distortion and self-deception. Theological diagnosis involves clarifying the issue so that the individual believer can see clearly and act on the basis of this clarity. This type of theological diagnosis, however, is careful to distinguish between clarification and simplification. While Farrer does not believe that the basic issues with which Christianity is concerned are ultimately enigmatic and paradoxical, he docs not assume that the simplest interpretation of an issue or problem is also the best clarification. One may distort an issue by oversimplifying it. The true test of a theological diagnosis of the problem is therefore not whether it has been made simple, but whether it has been made plain. The theological diagnosis has done its job if the listener can say, "Yes, now I am clear about this problem. Before, I was confused about it. Now, I can see it clearly." In Farrer's view, the Christian faith and the objective of clarity will always be allies in the diagnosis of a problem.

6. *Theological diagnosis as assessment of problems in terms of the deepest intentions of shared human experience.* In this type of sermon, the problem under review is held up to the mirror of our deepest kinds of human interaction. This diagnostic interpretation evaluates a problem in terms of our deepest aspirations for love, fidelity, courage, compassion. When this is done, the presumption is that the problem has been assessed from the perspective of the Christian faith. This type focuses on both *shared* human experience and private experiences that are commonly experienced by others. Through this emphasis on human experience that we share with others, the problem is viewed according to humanity's deepest social and communal intentions. There is the conviction of a fundamental congruity between the Christian faith and humanity's deepest capacities for mutuality and common enterprise.

Friedrich Schleiermacher's sermons are examples of this type of diagnosis.[40] In "Forgiveness and Love," Schleiermacher takes up Luke's account of the sinful woman who anointed Jesus' feet with ointment (Luke 7:36–50). He focuses on Jesus' statement, "I tell you that her sins, her many sins, must have been forgiven her, or she would not have shown such great love. It is the man who is forgiven little who shows little love." In reflecting on the relationship between forgiveness and love, Schleiermacher says that "experience teaches us" that it is our deficiency or lack of love which convicts us of our need for forgiveness. Conversely, when we find ourselves able to love, we know that divine forgiveness has begun its work in us. The restoration of our capacity to love is our strongest assurance that we have been forgiven.

But what about the parts of Jesus' statement that center on *degrees* of forgiveness? If there is a greater capacity to love in those who have been forgiven much, while there is a much lesser capacity to love among those who have been forgiven little, this would seem to imply that there is an advantage to having sinned much,

> as if grace could go forth most powerfully only on him in whom sin had been mightiest; as if he who, while still far from the life of God, was restrained, possibly by some mere external check, from plunging deep in the slough of sensuality, should now, as if in punishment of that abstinence, be able to attain only to a low degree of the spiritual life.

In Schleiermacher's view, this kind of reasoning fails to understand that the persons for whom *little* is forgiven are not those who have in fact sinned little, but those who still think lightly of their sins because they love little. This fact can be understood by viewing love and forgiveness in terms of the deepest intentions of shared human experience. If we look at our dearest and closest family relationships, we can hardly conclude, in comparison to the love that these relationships require of us, that we have sinned little and little has been forgiven us. Rather, these relationships, precisely because of the great demands for love they place on us, are the very relationships that require us to confess we have sinned much and require much forgiveness. As Schleiermacher puts it:

But he who requires of himself what the Spirit in His fulness can accomplish—and how much that is, the spirit of love alone can estimate; he who longs for the good of those whom God has given him just as he longs for his own; in a word, he who loves much;—oh, how often will he find cause to entreat for patience and forbearance; how deeply will he feel that to him much must be forgiven.

Thus, persons who want to show much love to other people will reproach themselves with many sins of omission, many moments of lazy indifference and cold reserve. In contrast, persons who have no intention of loving much, who say that their main concern is simply to avoid doing injury to anyone, feel there is little to be forgiven.

Here, Schleiermacher uses our shared human experience to clarify the relationship between love and forgiveness. He focuses on the deeper intentions of these shared experiences, especially as reflected in family relationships, to support his theological diagnosis. This diagnosis says that not only are love and forgiveness related in general terms; there are also correspondences between *degrees* of love and *degrees* of forgiveness. Love and forgiveness are shown to be much more precisely related when viewed in terms of our deepest communal intentions than when sin and forgiveness are viewed in purely individualistic terms.

Schleiermacher takes a similar diagnostic approach in "The Christian Training of Children." Here, he is concerned with the fact that the few references to child-rearing in the New Testament (Eph. 6:4 and Col. 3:21) warn parents against creating resentment in their children. Why this emphasis on not provoking children to resentment? Why is this issue so important? Schleiermacher explores this matter of not provoking resentment in children by viewing it in terms of parents' deep intentions for their children. Thus the Bible warns against provoking children to resentment because if children develop a resentful spirit toward their parents, they will mistrust the motives of their parents in every dimension of their relationship. They will respond to every action of the parents with bitterness and hostility. Then, none of the parents' deeper intentions toward the child will be realized.

On the other hand, if children do not develop this resentful attitude, their confidence in their parents' goodwill is itself a resource in their parents' efforts to provide the training they need to become productive and contented young adults:

> The whole being of the child is, in its very origin and essence, related to the parents; a thousand resemblances declare this to us in the most striking way; and it would seem inevitable that every new stage of the child's development must result in increasing love and unity of feeling. The child grows up in the closest connection with the parents; his earliest glance meets the loving eye of the mother; it is her notice that the first bright smile of the little one seeks to attract. The first lesson his mother teaches him is to know and love his father; and as the young minds expand, they cannot but feel more and more how everything comes to them from and through their parents. Here, therefore, is the inmost, inviolate sanctuary of love; and if here, in children, who are at first all clinging affection, there yet arises estrangement, anger, repugnance; if the love which can never be uprooted from their hearts, instead of being set on those who naturally and by God's appointment are nearest to them, turns away to other objects, so that they can bear from others what from their parents would embitter them; this is surely the most unnatural outcome that could be from the home training.

Also, if children develop an enduring resentment toward their parents, the parents are themselves deprived of the refreshment and strength that should come to them through their children. If the children "wait with closed hearts and painful suspense to see what kind of humor we are in," then we as parents are deprived of their "ingenuous frankness," and they "have only become an additional part of our anxiety and care." Thus, "When we provoke and estrange our children, both they and we lose the best of our life together." Here Schleiermacher's diagnosis focuses on shared experiences that reflect our deepest and most enduring communal intentions. The shared experiences that undergird our Christian faith are those that are aligned against interpersonal estrangements and conducive to increasing love.

Given Schleiermacher's emphasis on shared experiences of a deeply communal nature, it is not surprising that many of his theological diagnoses are based on family relations. But family relations are not the only instances of deep communal intentions. The Christian community, the neighborhood, the city, the nation as a whole reflect deep communal intent. In "Thanksgiving After Chastisement," preached at the end of a major cholera epidemic, Schleiermacher observes that the epidemic has raised some doubts about the value of the ordinary projects people committed themselves to before the outbreak. What is the value of these projects in the light of the recent disaster? Why not return to the simplest possible life "without so many exertions which yet may so easily be brought to mockery?" In dialectical fashion, however, Schleiermacher also observes that many have expressed the opposing viewpoint. They have argued that their former projects were never engaged in solely for enjoyment or vain pleasure, or merely to strive after possessions. Rather, they worked from a sense of faithfulness to their responsibility to cultivate the earth and bring it to perfection. Thus, "Why should the chastisement that has come upon us make the manner of life which we have inherited and continuously cultivated, in any way distasteful to us?"

In offering his own diagnosis of the problem Schleiermacher says that the second perspective is correct when it points out that something more than mere self-serving interest was involved in the community's enterprises prior to the epidemic. The people are therefore fully justified in resuming these tasks. On the other hand, he points out that the epidemic did demonstrate that they were capable of more deeds of love and faithfulness, that they could exercise greater moderation, and that they could marshal a kind of pious cheerfulness in the face of disaster. Thus, as they resume their previous enterprises, their recent shared experience tells them that these enterprises need to be leavened with an even greater sense of mutual commitment and love.

The fifth type of theological diagnosis sees a profound relationship between Christian truth and the objective of clarity. This type sees an equally profound relationship between the Christian faith and our deeper expressions of human community.

Types of Theological Diagnosis and Pastoral Counseling

How can these types of theological diagnosis be used in pastoral counseling? As we discuss their potential value to pastoral counseling, we should note that most if not all of these types are already explicitly used in pastoral counseling. Some of the counseling theories used by pastoral counselors reflect these diagnostic types. While these counseling theories may not affirm the theological emphases of these types of theological diagnosis, they may use some of the same diagnostic methods, identifying personal motives, exploring causes, exposing inadequate formulations of the problem, and so forth. Moreover, we will be able to show that certain types of theological diagnosis are similar to counseling methods in which the *diagnostic attitude* is especially prevalent, whereas other types are similar to methods in which *empathic understanding* is most valued.

As we discuss their potential value to pastoral counseling, we will be especially attentive to the ways in which these types can build on the diagnostic methods already employed in pastoral counseling.

1. *Identifying underlying personal motivations.* When employed in pastoral counseling this approach considers the problem to be largely motivational. Take, for example, the counselee who has a marital problem. The reconstruction of this problem may reveal that the marriage is foundering because one or both partners "want" it to fail. Quite likely, this desire is largely unconscious; it is not something that can be readily acknowledged. The counselee may be unaware that his parents' divorce when he was a young child is a

negative motivating factor in his own marriage. He may be saying on the surface, "I have tried hard to make my marriage work because my parents failed at theirs." But on a deeper level he may be communicating through attitudes deeper than words, "I have no right to succeed at something my parents failed at." While especially typical of traditional *psychoanalytic* counseling, this diagnostic approach is found in any pastoral counseling method that centers on personal motivation (e.g., the use of transactional analysis).

What makes the diagnosis of personal motivations a *theological* task? If we take a careful look at Newman's use of this diagnostic method, we can see that it is the enduring motivational direction of an individual life that matters. Also, the soundness of this motivational direction is determined by the degree to which it is consistent with *the will of God.* Thus, the theological role of the pastoral counselor is to encourage the counselee to reflect on this enduring motivational direction. Does this counselee assume that success in areas in which his own parents failed is something to feel guilty about? Is this guilt a factor not only in his marriage but also in his professional life, his personal friendships, and his relationships with his children? It would also be appropriate for the counselor, as practical theologian, to encourage the counselee to evaluate the motivational thrust of his life not only against standards of personal achievement but also in terms of God's will for his life. The question is not merely whether the counselee's guilt over success means the failure to live up to personal and social standards, but whether it is consistent with the will of God for his life. An underlying theological conviction of this emphasis on motivational structures is that, when we are genuinely open and responsive to the will of God, the motivational patterns of our lives can be changed and even transformed. Diagnosing one's underlying personal motivations in terms of God's will is the initial step in transforming these motivational structures.

2. *Identifying the range of potential causes.* Here the counselee's difficulties are located in their full psychosocial con-

text. In the case of the counselee who is having marital problems, a variety of possible contributing factors will be considered. Are the children or the in-laws contributing to the problem? Are financial difficulties involved? Does the couple have conflicting personal and professional goals? Are there problems in interpersonal communication or sexual adjustment? Is there evidence of psychological immaturity? Are differing economic, ethnic, or religious backgrounds involved? Is alcohol a contributing factor? Has there been prolonged separation because of military or other professional obligations? Is the husband or the wife gone from home for extended periods of time? These are just some of the vast range of possible causes of the counselee's marital problems. The diagnostic task is to identify the major contributing factors and to determine why these loom especially large in the counselee's marital difficulties. This type of diagnostic method is most common in counseling theories based on social psychology, social psychiatry, social work, and vocational counseling. It is also common in pastoral counseling theories that attribute the success or failure of marriages to one or more psychosocial factors (economic, communication skills, sexual adjustment, etc.), as in family counseling theory.

What makes this diagnosis a theological task? In his use of this type of theological diagnosis Wesley places heavy emphasis on *human responsibility,* both in the development of the problem and in the assessment of what can be done about it. Wesley resists the idea that God is the perpetrator of the problem, that God desires that we have this problem, or that God is indifferent about its outcome. To be sure, this responsibility may not rest solely with the counselee. Other individuals and various extenuating factors may also be responsible. But ultimate responsibility for our problems cannot be shifted onto God. In fact, by challenging the desire to ascribe responsibility to God, the counselor encourages the counselee to weigh the relative influence of other potential causes of the problem, and to determine to what extent the solution to the problem is within his control. Moreover, there is a greater possibility that the counselee will see that God might be an important factor in the resolution of the problem. What may appear on the surface to be evidence of God's desire to weigh us down with problems is more appropriately viewed as evidence of his desire to participate with us in the overcoming of these difficulties. As Wesley puts it, God's seeming withdrawal is actually his way of encouraging us to follow where he has gone. Thus, God has confidence in our capacity to take the kinds of initiatives that will justify this confidence.

3. *Exposing inadequate formulations of the problem.* There are times when the counselee comes to the counselor persuaded that the problem is one thing, and before long it turns out that the problem is something else. There are also instances when the counselee has identified the problem, but in the course of counseling begins to recognize that the problem is much more complex than originally thought. For example, the counselee may come to the counseling session persuaded that his marital problems are due to the fact that he and his wife have conflicting ideas about disciplining the children. But he discovers in the course of the counseling hour that he and his wife are vying for their children's affections. This type of diagnosis, therefore, questions inadequate assessments of the problem in order to open the way for a more penetrating view. Counseling based on theories of *depth psychology* is most likely to reflect this type of diagnostic method, because depth psychologies (e.g., Freudian, Jungian) seek to penetrate beneath surface explanations to deeper understandings of the problem.

What makes this diagnostic method theological? Tillich's sermons indicate that this method encourages individuals to risk relinquishing a superficial understanding of the issue and to open themselves to a deeper but less comforting view. A person is encouraged to take this risk because the deeper one goes in this exploration, the more one experiences the *underlying grace of God* and its upholding power. To take this risk does not mean that the problem will be more easily solved. It is easier, for example, to devise a solution for a couple's conflicting views on disciplining their children than to explore the interpersonal dynamics of their competition for their children's affections. Similarly, it may be easier to deal with these interpersonal dynamics than to explore the deeper self-images revealed by this competitive behavior. But taking this risk means that as counselees explore their problems at deeper and deeper levels, they become increasingly aware of the power of divine grace.

4. *Drawing attention to untapped personal and spiritual resources.* Counseling based on this approach recognizes that diagnosis involves discerning not only the nature and seriousness of the problem, but also the resources available for dealing with the problem. In the case of the counselee having marital problems, some of the available resources are personal, such as the counselee's willingness to come to grips with these problems, even if this requires significant changes in his own personality. Other resources are contextual, such as the availability of support groups, or his wife's willingness to participate in these counseling sessions. Counseling theories that focus on untapped personal resources are typically based on the principles of *humanistic psychology,* which emphasizes the individual's capacity for growth and self-fulfillment.

What makes this diagnostic method theological? Brooks's sermons indicate that this form of diagnosis is theological when it emphasizes recalling what God has done for us in the past. Such recollection is a source of hope and thus a significant spiritual resource. This *hope* enables the counselee to envision and work toward a more effective handling of his present difficulties. And because this hope is rooted in recalling God's faithfulness in the past, it is more than mere optimism. While optimism is based on the confidence that one has the personal capacities and contextual resources for dealing effectively with the problem, hope is based on the anticipation that even as God has been faithful in the past, so he will be faithful in the future. The counselee with marital problems may leave the session with greater hope for the future because he has been encouraged to recall previous experiences in his marriage when there were clear evidences of God's support. This type of theological diagnosis is based on the conviction that recalling God's support in the past will not cause individuals to succumb to helpless dependence on God, but will give them a new vision of how they can work together with God toward a more promising future. Thus, this spiritual resource of hope would inspire the counselee to avail himself of other personal and contextual resources that might otherwise be overlooked or neglected.

5. *Bringing clarity to the problem.* Counseling based on this form of diagnosis places considerable emphasis on eliminating distortions so that the problem can be seen for what it really is. This type of counseling is especially attentive to evidence of deception. The couple may be pretending that nothing is wrong between them, or they may be deceiving each other. While the truth is painful, the counselor encourages the counselee to face the truth because it is ultimately less painful than illusions, deceptions, and lies. Moreover, once the truth is acknowledged, it becomes a valuable ally in the counselee's efforts to deal with the problem. Numerous counseling theories focus on clarifying the problem. Psychoanalysis is concerned with eliminating illusion and self-deception. Client-centered therapy (especially in its earlier stages) places considerable emphasis on clarifying the counselee's experiences; also, reality therapy, values clarification therapies, and crisis counseling have stressed the importance of gaining a clearer picture of the problem and then devising a plan for coping with it.

What makes this diagnostic method theological? Farrer's sermons show that the elimination of distortion, illusion, and self-deception is never simply a psychological or philosophical endeavor. The goal of seeing the problem in its true light is itself a moral and spiritual task. This is because to replace confusion with clarity is to participate in God's creative work. By nature, God prefers *truth* to deception, light to darkness, clarity to illusion, revelation to concealment. Thus, counseling based on this type of theological diagnosis encourages the counselee to understand that, in discovering the truth, one is also discovering how God is at work in one's life. If the truth is ultimately not as painful as deception, this is because the truth reveals God's own role in the ordering of one's life.

6. *Assessing problems in terms of the deepest intentions of shared human experience.* Counseling based on this diagnostic method stresses the importance of the counselee's own experience. While many people have marital problems, this particular counselee experiences these marital problems in his own unique way. Wayne E. Oates suggests that there are several typical stages in the process of marital separation, including (1) unilateral decision-making; (2) mutual deception; (3) withdrawal into dispair; (4) involvement of other people in the separation; (5) physical and social separation; (6) legal divorce; (7) post-divorce bereavement.[41] While the pastoral counselor can make effective use of this analysis of the process of marital separation, this type of diagnostic method would focus on the counselee's unique experience in relation to this process. How does it feel to *this* counselee to be the victim of deception? How does *this* counselee experience withdrawal into despair? The counselor's task here is to attempt to understand the counselee's marital problems as the counselee uniquely experiences them, not as "most people" experience them. This means entering into the counselee's own internal frame of reference and sharing in this experience. It is the client-centered approach (especially in its later phases) that places particular emphasis on this type of diagnostic method. However, Rogers points out that accomplished representatives of other psychotherapeutic schools also place a high premium on the importance of understanding the problem from the perspective of the counselee's own experience.[42] Thus, this type of diagnostic method is not limited to the client-centered approach.

What makes this diagnostic method theological? Schleiermacher's sermons point to the importance of diagnosing human problems in terms of the deepest intentions of *shared* human experience. Thus, as the counseling session focuses on the uniquely personal experience of the counselee, this experience is evaluated in the light of our capacities for deep and enduring commitment to one another. "What is most personal is most general." The counselee's unique experience of marital difficulties can be assessed, for example, in terms of humanity's deepest capacity for forgiveness and love. The theological diagnosis encourages the counselee to consider his experiences in the light of these capacities. This may prompt the counselee to acknowledge his failure to act toward his wife in terms of these deepest intentions, and it may open the possibility of deeper experiences of forgiveness and love in the future. Or the counselee may recognize that the deeper intentions of shared human experience are best served by terminating this marriage. In either case, diagnosis assesses the counselee's present experience in terms of the deeper levels of shared experience to which humanity aspires. This method is theological in that these aspirations reflect the profound depths of *God's love toward us.*

Conclusion

To conclude our discussion of how these six types of theological diagnosis can inform counseling, note that each type of theological diagnosis emphasizes a different dimension of our relationship to God. The first type stresses the will of God for one's life. The second stresses God's encouragement of human responsibility and initiative. The third emphasizes the experience of the grace of God. The fourth stresses the constructive role of hope in God. The fifth emphasizes the place of truth in our relation to God. The sixth stresses the communal dimensions of our relation to God, especially in the form of active love. Thus, in each case, problems encountered in counseling are diagnosed in the light of an important dimension of our relationship to God.[43]

Does this mean that the counselor needs to say to the counselee at some point in the counseling session: "Let us consider your problem in terms of your relationship to God. What does this relationship have to say to your problem?" First, if we take the *sermon* as our model for the communication of theological diagnoses, we should note that the effective sermon does not introduce these diagnoses in a clumsy or stereotypical fashion. Similarly, the counselor should not be flatfooted or arbitrary in diagnosing the problem theologically.

Secondly, the general style and tone of the theological diagnosis has already been established in the *reconstruction stage* of the counseling process. Each of the six types of theological diagnosis reconstructs the problem in a different way. The first type reconstructs it in motivational terms. The second reconstructs it in terms of psychosocial factors, and so forth. In each case, the basic contours of the theological diagnosis are already being formed in the reconstruction stage. Diagnosis of the problem in the face of our relationship to God is therefore communicated within the parameters of the chosen mode of reconstruction.

On the basis of these two points, we can say that theological diagnoses are not simply a matter of announcing to counselees that their problems must be viewed in terms of their relationship to God. Effective theological diagnosis in pastoral counseling manifests the same sensitivity to verbal subtlety and precision that the preacher employs in the sermon. In addition, the form that this theological diagnosis takes will depend to a significant degree on the manner in which the reconstruction of the problem has itself been shaped and formed.

One final issue that we need to take up is that of empathic understanding: Do some of these types of theological diagnosis reflect the diagnostic attitude and others reflect empathic understanding? While much depends on how the individual counselor employs these types, it would be fair to say that the first type most reflects *external* diagnosis because it emphasizes motivation of which the listeners are largely unconscious. The type that most reflects *empathic understanding* is the sixth type, with its emphasis on the counselee's own process of experiencing. The other four types reflect various shadings in between. Type two identifies the major determinants of the problem from a preestablished set of typical personal and social factors. While type three does not attempt to predetermine where the exploration of the problem will lead, it assumes that this exploration will involve a predictable progression from surface to depth. The counseling process in types four and five are not as structured. Type four assumes the existence of positive resources for dealing with the problem, but does not presume to know in advance what these might be. Similarly, type five focuses on clarification of the problem, but has no set pattern or preestablished assumptions about how clarity is to be achieved.

Thus, as we move from type one to type six, we can detect less imposition of a set conceptual schema on the diagnostic interpretation and a greater tendency to allow the problem itself to shape the diagnosis. The first three types are more likely to apply the diagnostic method with less variation regardless of the problem being addressed. The latter three types are more likely to allow the problem to structure the diagnosis. We might say that the diagnosis in the first three types follows a more deductive pattern, and in the latter three, a more inductive pattern. It should be emphasized, however, that there is no guarantee that certain types will reflect a more empathic approach while others will necessarily enforce a more diagnostic attitude. All that can appropriately be said is that, other things being equal, the sixth type of theological diagnosis is more conducive to a counseling atmosphere of empathic understanding than is the first type. But "other things being equal" is a large qualification. The particular skills and sensitivities of the counselor, the nature and intensity of the counselee's investment in the counseling, and the quality of the interpersonal relationship between counselor and counselee, are all significant nondiagnostic factors in determining whether the session will reflect empathic understanding or not.

It should also be noted that the differences between the six types of theological diagnosis *in regard to empathic understanding* are relative. It would be quite wrong to say that the first type lacks any empathic understanding while the sixth type is a perfect example of such understanding.

The sermons from which these types have been drawn would belie any judgment of this sort. For example, Newman's capacity to preach to his congregation with empathic understanding is clearly reflected in the closing paragraph of the last sermon he preached as an Anglican clergyman, "The Parting of Friends":

> And, O my brethren, O kind and affectionate hearts, O loving friends, should you know any one whose lot it has been, by writing or by word of mouth, in some degree to help you thus to act; if he has ever told you what you knew about yourselves, or what you did not know; has read to you your wants or feelings, and comforted you by the very reading; has made you feel that there was a higher life than this daily one, and a brighter world than that you see; or encouraged you, or sobered you, or opened a way to the enquiring, or soothed the perplexed; if what he has said or done has ever made you take interest in him, and feel well inclined towards him; remember such a one in time to come, thought you hear him not, and pray for him, that in all things he may know God's will, and at all times he may be ready to fulfil it.[44]

While insisting here that he had always sought to carry out his diagnostic responsibilities to his parishioners, Newman also notes that he tried to do this with a genuinely empathic understanding of his listeners. We may conclude that, even as the best therapists place a high premium on empathic understanding regardless of their chosen counseling theory, so also the best preachers place a high value on empathic understanding, whatever their chosen form of theological diagnosis.

A final disclaimer. My concern here is not to sell the reader on one or another of these diagnostic methods. These are merely examples of the diagnostic use of theology in preaching. On the other hand, I do believe that pastors should establish some consistency in the use of diagnostic methods in their preaching and counseling. I doubt that one can be effective in pastoral counseling, at least in the long run, if the diagnostic method employed in one's counseling differs radically from the diagnostic method employed in one's preaching. If an integrated ministry is a desirable professional goal, achieving such consistency in diagnostic method is a matter of high priority.

Chapter 5

Proclamation in Pastoral Counseling

Let's now turn from diagnosis to proclamation. We have linked preaching and pastoral counseling through their commitment to diagnosis. But a central purpose of preaching, perhaps *the* central purpose, is proclamation. Is this also a purpose of pastoral counseling? Can we say that preaching and pastoral counseling are integrated if the one does not share the central purpose of the other?

The idea that proclamation of the gospel is central to pastoral counseling is usually resisted by pastoral theologians. They are worried, and justifiably so, that pastors might view this as a license to "preach at" their counselees. They have argued, therefore, that it is not what the counselor says, but the relationship between the counselor and counselee, that communicates the fundamental affirmations of the Christian faith. Proclamation of the gospel is reserved for the pulpit.

The problem with this approach is that pastors in their counseling have relied on this relationship to make whatever affirmation of the Christian faith they deem appropriate, and have used "secular" psychotherapies as their primary medium of verbal communication. They have therefore not had a very clear sense that pastoral counseling has a Christian purpose. Certainly, they have not felt that a major purpose of pastoral counseling is to proclaim the Christian gospel.

How, then, can pastoral counseling become a proclamatory event similar to preaching? In addressing this question, we need to take seriously the view, made popular in the 1950's and 1960's, that basic affirmations of the Christian faith can be communicated through the *relationship* of counselor and counselee. The argument that proclamation can occur in pastoral counseling needs to take this view seriously. We would not want to restore the proclamatory function of counseling at the expense of gains that have been made toward identifying what makes a good counseling relationship.

Biblical Models in Pastoral Counseling

In Chapter 1 we mentioned John Cobb's call for pastoral counseling that is responsive to the need to "bring our language-world and that of the Bible together." Were this to occur in counseling, it would set the stage for proclamation of the Christian faith through the Biblical witness to that faith. Unfortunately, there is considerable confusion today about how the Bible might be employed in pastoral counseling without doing violence to the Bible or the counseling relationship. Cobb freely acknowledges that his own discussion does not go much beyond calling for more attention to the role of Biblical thought structures in pastoral counseling. What follows is an attempt to restore the proclamatory function of pastoral counseling by identifying specific ways in which Biblical thought might inform pastoral counseling. Our discussion focuses on three Biblical models of pastoral counseling. I call these three models the *psalmic,* the *proverbic,* and the *parabolic.* They are based on the perspectives of psalms, proverbs and parables. I will pay particular attention to the *parabolic* model because, in my view, it holds the most promise for recovering the proclamatory purpose of pastoral counseling.[45]

The Psalmic Model of Pastoral Counseling

The psalmic model of pastoral counseling was the dominant Biblical model in the 1950's and 1960's. It was supported by the enormous popularity of Carl Rogers' client-centered counseling method. While best articulated in Seward Hiltner's influential book, *Pastoral Counseling*,[46] it found its way into most of the major books on pastoral counseling during this period. I call it the psalmic model because, like the psalms, it places particular emphasis on emotions and feelings. Many psalms express profound discouragement, frustration, bewilderment, anger, despair; while many others express happiness, joy, relief, gratitude. The counselor's task in this model of pastoral counseling is to empathize with the *feelings* of the counselee. This normally involves understanding that the counselee's emotions are conflicted. One set of emotions conflicts with another set; thus both love and anger may be directed toward the same individual. In a similar way, psalms often express conflicting emotions toward friends, enemies, or God.

The psalmic model also takes the view that the counselor's task is not to moralize or to offer general or conventional explanations as to why the counselee is suffering. Rather, the counselor's task is to be understanding and responsive, to "be there" and "suffer with" the counselee. Again, the client-centered method is similar to the psalms. It does not rely on active efforts to intervene in an individual's plight, but instead depends on the therapeutic value of communicating feelings to an understanding person. The psalms do not offer specific explanations for an individual's plight. Their efficacy results from communicating one's distress, often with considerable attention to making one's words fit the emotions felt at the time.

The Psalms are often alluded to in the pastoral counseling literature produced under the influence of the client-centered approach. Hiltner's *Pastoral Counseling* has eight pages on the use of the Bible in pastoral counseling. Nearly six are devoted to a counseling case that involved exploring a parishioner's feelings of depression in the light of the Thirty-eighth Psalm.[47] In his efforts to help this counselee understand his feelings of depression, the pastor noted that his parishioner and the psalmist had similar feelings. In describing the stages in the psalmist's lament, he points out that the psalmist first "faces the fact of how he feels. He doesn't just say, 'I feel bad, but I know I shouldn't; therefore I don't.' He admits it. He even tells himself that he had tried to overlook the facts for a long time; he was like a deaf man or a dumb man. He had thought he could get along by being perfect, never letting his foot slip. But that didn't help. So next he realizes there must be something about himself, his own sin. So he tells the Lord he is a sinner. But in the next breath he says his enemies follow evil, while he actually follows good. He asks the Lord not to forsake him. He feels he is a good man, though a sinner, but he still feels alone." The counselee immediately responds to the pastor's emphasis on the "feeling" level of the psalm: "That's certainly the way it goes all right. I hadn't thought of that. There is a regular series of steps he takes. But he doesn't really get anywhere. He may be courageous in admitting how he feels, but what good does it do? He feels just as bad at the end as he did at the beginning, doesn't he?" Here the psalm is used as a means of eliciting reflection on the counselee's own feelings.

Another example of the psalmic model in pastoral counseling is Carroll Wise's *Psychiatry and the Bible*.[48] While Wise uses many portions of the Bible, his use of the Psalms establishes his primary concern with feelings. In his discussion of Psalm 38, the same psalm that Hiltner uses, he points out that "In this psalm we are dealing with conflicting feelings about God. On the one side he punishes; on the other, he understands and even participates in suffering. Many people have similar conflicting feelings about God. By facing and examining such feelings we may gain insight into ourselves and into the experiences out of which these feelings grow."

Here, Wise emphasizes examination of one's conflicting feelings to gain insight into oneself.

The Proverbic Model of Pastoral Counseling

The proverbic model of pastoral counseling emerged in the early 1970's. It was a reaction against the psalmic model, which it considered "too passive" or "too neutral" or "too nondirective." It appeared when more "active" psychotherapeutic theories, such as reality therapy and various behavior modification therapies, were emerging. Its most vigorous proponent has been Jay E. Adams, who develops the proverbic model (he calls it the "nouthetic" model) in his book *Competent to Counsel.*[49] Adams is critical of client-centered counseling because the counselor refuses to give advice to the counselee, emphasizes acceptance rather than admonishment, stresses moral neutrality rather than moral judgment, advocates listening to the feeling level beneath the verbal content rather than the verbal content itself, and emphasizes feelings and emotions to the neglect of behaving, acting, and doing. In direct opposition to client-centered counseling, Adams' nouthetic approach to pastoral counseling emphasizes admonishment and advice-giving.

While he believes this approach is consistent with the Bible as a whole, Adams says that the proverbs are the best example of nouthetic counseling. In criticizing what he takes to be the value neutrality of client-centered counseling, he suggests that "judgments of moral value in counseling are precisely what the Scriptures everywhere commend," and then cites the proverbs as the Bible's example of moral judgment. He writes: "Moral judgment is the essence of counsel in the book of Proverbs. The unique element in the wisdom of that counsel is its moral orientation. These are commands for the covenant people which enable them to live in proper covenant relationship to God." Adams concludes that Proverbs is "a book of directive counseling," one that gives particular attention to the counselor's role as a parental guide. He points out that nouthetic counselors frequently hand individual portions of Proverbs to their counselees. They do this because the proverbs give wise counsel, reproof, and discipline.

If the psalmic model of pastoral counseling stresses feelings, the proverbic model emphasizes behavioral change. As Adams puts it, "Proverbs assumes the need for divine wisdom imparted (as in nouthetic counseling) by verbal means: by instruction, by reproof, by rebuke, by correction, and by applying God's commandments in order to change behavior for one's benefit." Also, because Proverbs exhorts individuals, especially young persons, to listen to others rather than depend on their own ideas, nouthetic counseling does not encourage counselees to do most of the talking. Instead, "counselors frequently ought to urge clients to listen to words of advice. The counselee needs to listen to words of counsel, reproof, commandment and instruction. That he has not done so in the past, may be one major cause of his present distress."

The Parabolic Model of Pastoral Counseling

The parabolic model is not easily identified with any existing approach to pastoral counseling. It has been employed in pastoral counseling, but with little explicit recognition that it is being used. Nor has there been much systematic reflection on this model in the literature. The major exceptions are James E. Dittes' *The Church in the Way, Minister on the Spot,* and *When the People Say No.* [50] While not explicitly designed to illustrate the use of the parabolic model in pastoral counseling, his books reflect the parabolic model. They are filled with "living parables"—such as a church board that cannot decide whether to spend some unexpected income in refurbishing the pastor's study or to contribute to the salary of a minister working in a low-rent housing project; a Bible study class that persists in resisting the assigned topic; a deacon who has great difficulty in following the Communion distribution procedure; a junior high Sunday school class that practices the Biblical injunction to "turn the other cheek"; a minister and board of elders who explore their attitudes about home visitation.

While Dittes does not refer to these examples as parables, there can be little doubt that they are influenced by the parable form. Sometimes Jesus' own parables are alluded to. In *The Church in the Way,* he discusses the case of a Sunday school teacher who had been disheartened when two boys disrupted a carefully planned dramatization of the parable of the prodigal son by breaking from the group and wrestling in the corner. As she reflected on this "disciplinary problem," she "suddenly discovered—with an audible 'aha'—that she had a real-life 'play within a play' right there in her room." In this case, Jesus' parable is a source of insight into the relevance of the boys' behavior to the lesson, and it therefore contributes to the teacher's change of attitude toward such behavior. Now, instead of viewing it as merely disruptive, she sees this behavior as a "meaningful" example of the point she hoped to make in the dramatization. In a similar way, Dittes' comparison of preaching in *The Minister on the Spot* to four ways of going out on a limb (guaranteed soft landing, clinging to the guaranteed limb, freedom as obligation, and assurance is in the breaking) is reminiscent of Jesus' parable of the four soils.

In his most recent book, *When the People Say No,* Dittes does not discuss Jesus' own parables but he treats the Biblical account of Peter and John's encounter with the beggar at the Beautiful Gate as a parable of healing. This story is an instance of how we can "see through" our customary expectations to find healing and transformative change. The account says that Peter fixed his eyes on the man and that, in turn, the man was all attention because he expected a gift from Peter and John. But, "When Peter looked at the man, what did he see? He saw a beggar, yes. He also saw a cripple. He also saw a whole man. To fix his eyes on *him,* to see him wholly, to minister to him, Peter needed to see all three." In seeing the man whole, Peter also saw through the man's own expectations and turned the episode at the Beautiful Gate from mere almsgiving to an act of healing.

Dittes has interpreted the events at the Beautiful Gate as a living parable. His reconstruction of this story as an instance of "seeing through expectations to find ministry" focuses on the distinctive features of the parable. These include:

1. The parable depicts an event whose meaning is not immediately obvious to the listeners. Something "happens" in the parable which typically results in an *altered relationship* between the participants in the event. After this event, their relationship is permanently altered.

2. The meaning of this event is communicated *through the story itself, especially its details.* While the early church sometimes added aphoristic statements to the parable in order to fix its meaning, the parable's meaning is not something that is added on, but is woven into the narrative.

3. The parable is *open-ended.* It does not "end" with the telling of the story. Thus, it does not eliminate the sense of life's ambiguity, it actually enhances it. Those who have no place for life's inherent ambiguities, uncertainties, and puzzling features in their religious vision will tend to give the parable low priority. The parable perceives life as filled with complex and risky decisions.

4. The parable emphasizes *insight* as a means of changing lives. Not only do characters in the story achieve "insight" about themselves (for example, the prodigal son "came to himself"), but the parable challenges listeners to gain new insight about themselves, the world, and God.

5. The parable is *transformative* because it culminates in the restructuring of perceptions. It reverses one's customary ways of perceiving the situations of life, challenging one to look at them in a wholly different light.[51]

Dittes touches on each of these characteristics in his discussion of the Beautiful Gate story. He notes the *altered relationship* between Peter and John, the beggar and the bystanders, as a result of Peter's perception of the needs that lay behind the man's expectations. He considers the *details* of this account to be important, details such as Peter fixing his eyes on the beggar and seeing there what others had failed to see. He sees the story as *open-ended* in the sense that Peter and John see through the man's expectations to his deeper needs and thus completely alter his future. Dittes also notes that the story involves *insight,* in that Peter perceives that the man is not just a beggar but a cripple and a whole person with needs that go beyond his request for alms. And the event is *transformative,* in that Peter's perception of these deeper needs resulted in an act of healing. By reflecting each of these characteristics of the parabolic form, Dittes' interpretation of this Biblical story is itself in the parabolic mode.

This parabolic model is not easily identified with any existing pastoral counseling method. Unlike proponents of the psalmic and proverbic models, Dittes does not attempt to develop a pastoral counseling method based on the parabolic mode. Still, in the practice of pastoral care and counseling, the model is familiar. Hospital visits written up in verbatim form have often been used as living parables from which one can learn to minister more effectively. Using the action-reflection model, such cases are often discussed as one might explore a parable: The case is an event that involves a *relationship* between the minister and the person being helped. Discussion often centers on how this relationship was altered in the course of the visit or how it can be altered in subsequent encounters. The verbatim is examined closely, because the meaning of the event is in its *details.* The case is considered *open-ended* because it is believed that effects of the experience will reach beyond the actual encounter. The case is scrutinized for evidence that the patient achieved *insight* conducive to real changes in perception about self, others, or God. In consequence of this insight, the case is potentially *transformative,* both of the patient and of the minister. Pastors can often point to one or two important "cases" that have transformed their own personal self-understanding and professional aspirations.

A good illustration of the parabolic model is the following case made available by Seward Hiltner and recently reprinted in Henri Nouwen's *Creative Ministry*. [52] This case includes all the characteristics of the parable: it protrays an altered relationship; it has meaning in small details; it is open-ended, conducive to insight, and potentially transformative.

Michael, dressed in a white coat like the medical interns but with a name tag identifying him as a chaplain, entered Mr. Kern's room for a pastoral visit. There the following conversation took place:

Mr. Kern: You're a new one. I don't believe I've seen you among the doctors.

Michael: You haven't, I'm sure, though I have been meaning to call on you sooner. I should have been here sooner than this. I am one of the chaplains, Chaplain Smith.

Mr. Kern: How do you do.

Michael: I just want to say Hello to you. I want to let you know that we're around and that we'll be happy to help in any way we can. The chaplain's office answers on extension 2765, and in case you are interested, there are services here on Sunday —several ecumenical and one Mass for Catholics.

Mr. Kern: I am Jewish.

Michael: Oh, fine. In that event you may be interested to know that though he is not here daily, a Rabbi makes regular visits here at Stone Memorial. Could I call him for you?

Mr. Kern: Please do not. I would prefer not to bother him —or anyone.

Michael: If you wish—How ill have you been?

Mr. Kern: Enough to die, but I don't! And all this doctoring has done and does no good—a continual torture. But I do not care to talk. Will you please excuse me?

Michael: I'm sure that I have come in at a very inopportune time, and I hope that I have not disturbed or upset you. Still, I would like to drop in from time to time, if for no other reason than to say Hello, just to see how things are with you.

Mr. Kern: You would indeed be doing me a very great favor

—and would be respecting my wishes perfectly, as I have told the doctors—if you and everyone else would leave me entirely alone. My own family, except for my wife, does not come to see me. I have told my daughter not to come. I don't want her to see me in this condition. Yet people insist. Even a dying animal —a dying animal—can crawl off by itself to die. I repeat: You will be doing me a favor if you leave—and do not return.

Back at his room Michael wrote: "I feel discouraged, even guilty. It was almost as if I had been kicked in the stomach."

Cases like this have been used by chaplain supervisors to disabuse students of any easy confidence in their capacity to minister effectively. As Nouwen points out, this case raises searching questions regarding one's pastoral *identity*, one's pastoral *relationship* with the person one is trying to help, and one's pastoral *approach*. These important pastoral issues all come to focus in this brief but extremely meaningful encounter between a young student-minister and a sick man. But as Michael and his pastoral colleagues reflect on the case, they will undoubtedly focus on the major characteristics of the parable. The case involves an event in which the relationship between the two participants undergoes significant alteration in the course of their conversation. This alteration is not all negative. The meaning of the case is in the small details of the communication between Michael and Mr. Kern, especially those embedded in Mr. Kern's final statements about his wife and daughter and his concern about his physical appearance. The encounter is open-ended in that Michael has reason to believe that he ministered to Mr. Kern and may have another opportunity to do so. The event is conducive to insight leading to perceptual restructuring. Mr. Kern's final statement about his physical appearance suggests that he is struggling with his perception of self and others. And, hopeless as it now seems, the experience is potentially transformative if Michael can "see through" Mr. Kern's meager expectations from this relationship and minister to his needs.

The Methods of the Three Counseling Models

Having identified these three Biblically informed models of pastoral counseling, I would now like to look more closely at the counseling methods that emerge from them. I will give most attention to the parabolic model because I believe that its emphasis on perceptual restructuring provides an excellent basis for proclamation in counseling.

The *proverbic* model is deliberately and self-consciously directive. It is based on admonition and advice. For this reason, it is a method that, according to Adams, is particularly well-suited to counseling the late adolescent or early young adult. Whether this directive approach is always the best for counseling this age group is open to question. The point is that the proverbic model emphasizes parental guidance to younger persons.

In direct contrast to the proverbio model, the *psalmic* model is nondirective. This model is based on the view that counselees have their own sense of direction. The counselor may clarify, assess, and even help toward the diagnosis of the counselee's problem, but the counselee is ultimately responsible for coming to some resolution of the problem. While this model has been used with a variety of age groups, it seems best suited to the young adult who is exploring feelings about marriage, about raising a family, formation of a profession and clarification of life's goals. Carl Rogers' own cases, for example, are typically of women and men in their twenties and thirties, struggling with the basic commitments of young adulthood. With such counselees, it seems appropriate for the counselor to invite the counselee to give the process its direction because the counselee needs a context in which to explore these commitments in relative freedom. For persons who raise searching questions about the various commitments they are making, the counseling session ought to be a context in which they are free to explore their feelings about such commitments in an open and nonthreatening atmosphere.

The *parabolic* model falls somewhere between the proverbic and psalmic models in terms of method. Like Jesus' use of stories to draw attention to the Kingdom of God, it is essentially indirective. Suggestions are made in a spirit of exploration rather than admonishment. Words of advice are offered seriously but tentatively, not in a spirit of demand or reproof. Because it is indirective, this model seems most appropriate in ministering to middle adults. While the directive approach may work well with the late adolescent, it assumes an authority-dependency relationship that cannot be assumed in the relationship of the pastor and the middle adult. While the nondirective approach seems particularly appropriate in the case of young adults who are sensitive about encroachments on their freedom and independence, such sensitivity need not be assumed of the middle adult. Thus, the pastor can be somewhat more direct, even as the parable itself has an element of directness. But this is a directness that assumes a common rapport between pastor and counselee, a sense that the two of them are much more alike than different, and that they understand each other in ways that make it unnecessary to engage in strongly directive language.

The indirective style of counseling can be illustrated by comparing typical family conversations. There are some strongly directive statements ("watch out for that car!") and some intentionally nondirective conversations ("I'm not asking for your opinion, I just want to let off some steam"). But the majority of family conversations are indirective ("If it will relieve your mind to see the doctor, then by all means go ahead and make an appointment"). One suspects that families function best if there is a preponderance of such indirective verbal communications over the directive and nondirective. Like nondirective forms of counseling, indirective conversations are *open-ended* and *insight-oriented*. But they are more concerned about discerning where the conversation might make an imperceptible shift toward *transformation*. They are like the parable that begins by supporting our expectations but then changes midway through the story into a different modality. Such changes often occur in nondirective counseling, and real transformations occur. But the indirective method is especially attentive to shifts and transitions in the counselee's narrative. It attempts to avoid the monotony of some nondirective counseling (this is not true of Rogers' own cases) where there is so much concern about the individual units of verbal interchange that these transitional points are missed.

Put another way, nondirective counseling is often more like the litany which has a basis in the psalm, than it is like the parable. Like the litany, nondirective counseling is superb in its responsive dimension. The left side of the congregation responds to the right side of the congregation and the appropriateness of its response moves the litany forward. As the litany proceeds, it becomes evident that it has a major theme —repentance, joy, and celebration, or service to the world. Given the antiphonal structure of the litany, there is more concern with the pattern of response than with the task of transforming the structure. Without minimizing the importance of this responsive pattern, the parabolic model is more attentive to structural gaps in the counselee's narrative because these gaps invite structural transformations.

A related difference between these two types of pastoral counseling is the nondirective model's emphasis on exploration of feelings and the indirective model's stress on *perception* and *perceptual restructurings*. Both types are open-ended and insight-oriented. But indirective counseling pays greater attention to points in the dialogue that suggest shifts toward perceptual restructuring, including the restructuring of one's self-perceptions and one's perceptions about the world or about God. This emphasis is due to the parabolic model's view that transformation (especially among middle adults) is fundamentally a matter of change in perception. As the parable unfolds, the listener begins to realize that this is not merely an interesting story. Rather, it is a story that lays a particular claim on its listeners. If one really "hears" the parable, one's life will necessarily change. Indeed, it will undergo a massive restructuring. And this restructuring is largely *perceptual* in nature. While the parable may evoke changes in feelings or changes in overt behavior, the restructuring is mainly one of perception. One sees oneself, one's neighbor, and one's world through different lenses.

A good illustration is the Rubin vase popularized by classical Gestalt psychology. Looked at one way, it is a vase. Looked at another way, it is a pair of individuals facing each other. The shift from viewing it as a vase to viewing it as a pair of faces is a perceptual restructuring. The one view of "reality" is totally negated in the other view of "reality." One cannot have it both ways at any given time.

In contrast to the perceptual shifts that occur when one is viewing the Rubin vase, the kind of restructuring that the parables effect can be more lasting. One's perception of self, others, and the world do not shift back and forth from one's pre-parabolic to one's post-parabolic perceptions. When the kind of reality that the parables point to is "seen" for what it is, it is most difficult to continue to understand oneself (as perceiver) and the world (as the perceived) as though this insight had never occurred. One's first encounter with urban slums or severe mental disorders is likely to produce a major shift in one's perception of self and world (and perhaps of the God who governs this world). This change is likely to have a permanent effect even if there is little indication of this change in one's behavior or even one's expression of feelings.

An example of a permanent perceptual restructuring is the following pastoral experience: The pastor spends the night in the hospital with a church elder whose wife is dying. The pastor and elder had been on friendly terms, but their relationship was rather casual. Now, as a result of this experience of keeping vigil, the elder sees the pastor in a wholly new light. They are now friends, a special bond exists between them. Six months later, when some of the other elders are discussing the possibility of asking for the pastor's resignation because they do not like his approach to evangelism, this parishioner squelches their conversation with the comment, "I'm not sure I like his evangelistic fervor any more than you do. But that man showed his true colors when he stayed up with me all through the night when Dorothy passed away. There is no way that I could join in any effort to force his resignation." A perceptual restructuring has taken place. The elder "sees" his pastor in a new light. Moreover, the restructuring is permanent. He simply cannot act against this new perception of his pastor.

There are cases in which the new perception is relinquished because subsequent experiences prove it to have been false. In this example, the pastor would have had to do things to directly negate the elder's perception that he was a genuinely caring individual. This could not have happened, however, merely because his views on evangelism were suspect. There would have to be actions that directly assaulted the parishioner's perception of the pastor as a man who cared about others. If such actions had happened, we would say that the elder was "disillusioned"—his perception of the pastor as one who genuinely cared for others would be proven false. However, that such disillusionment could occur only under special circumstances is testimony to the fact that perceptual restructurings can be permanent. The elder in this case cannot "see" the pastor in the way he saw him before, or in the way some of the other elders "see" him now.

Perception is also important to the relationship between counselor and counselee in the parabolic model. The helping persons in Jesus' own parables—the good Samaritan, the father in the parable of the prodigal son, the vineyard owner in the parable of the laborers in the vineyard, or the judge in the parable of the judge and the importunate widow—are all perceptive individuals. They perceive needs, they perceive the thoughts behind an individual's words, and they perceive the consequences of their own actions toward the other individual. While different in their "helping" styles, they share the same capacity to discern the potential for change inherent in the situation. The Gospel writers also tell us that Jesus was extremely perceptive. He would listen to the "parables" of others—the father whose son could not speak, the woman at the well, the woman who anointed his feet with oil, and persons who told their stories under the influence of demons —and he would immediately perceive both the need and the possibility of transformation implicit in the story.

Proclamation Through Perceptual Restructuring

The following diagram schematizes much of what has been said about these three Biblical models of pastoral counseling. Each model is a legitimate approach. Each has its strengths and weaknesses as a counseling method. But given our interest in the proclamatory function of pastoral coun-

Biblical Models of Pastoral Counseling

Model	Method	Focus of Change	Paradigmatic Counselee
Proverbic	directive	behavior	adolescent
Psalmic	nondirective	feelings	young adult
Parabolic	indirective	perception	middle adult

seling, the parabolic model merits special attention. It addresses Barth's view that proclamation involves helping listeners "see" what is in fact the case. It also enables us to address the polarization of "proclamation" and "relationship" evident in discussions about directive vs. nondirective methods. The indirective approach shares the directive counselor's respect for "proclamation" and the nondirective counselor's emphasis on "relationship." Thus, it seeks to make the counseling session a proclamatory event

while fostering a relationship between counselor and counselee of empathic understanding.

In indirective counseling, the goal is perceptual restructuring. The means to this goal is proclamation, especially as
reflected in the parable. To illustrate this link between proclamation and perception, let us consider further the case of the
guilt-ridden parishioner introduced in Chapter 3 (from Cryer
and Vayhinger, *Casebook in Pastoral Counseling*).

When we left the case, John had just told the pastor that
he expected God to punish him, not out of hatred toward
him, but simply because "there are certain things when you
do something wrong you have to pay for it." He then proceeds with an account of how his parents' punishment of him
for things he had done wrong was immediate and fair, and
this served to clear the air between them:

Pastor: Punishment rather than hate?

John: Yeah. Like when you add numbers up, you get so
many and that's it. You add up punishment and
you get so many and something has to happen.
Then you wipe the slate clean. Take for example,
at home. I remember when I was small, my mother
she loved me, my father loved me too, and we were
happy at home. They used to do everything for me
all the time. I used to go out and play and then
when they'd call me I wouldn't come some time.
Like I remember one time, there was a field behind
our house, and we always went out and played
football. This one night I remember, I was out there
playing. Mother called me for supper, but I didn't
come. I heard her, but I didn't want to leave the
game. I was playing, and it was important that we
win. We had the ball; so I stayed there until the
game was over. Then when I got home they knew
I heard. I got a licking, went to bed. All they gave
me was a glass of milk. It's the same thing with

God. You see they loved me too; but because I
didn't come home, because I was bad, I broke the
law of obeying a parent, I had to pay. I had to go
to bed. And the next morning when I got up everything was okay. But he's making me wait. I'm willing to pay, I'm willing to get sick or something, I
don't know. He's making me wait. But the thing is
bothering me. I can't wait any longer. I must—got
to have something done.

Pastor: You feel that you have to be punished by God as
you are punished by others; but the waiting for this
punishment is bothering you a great deal—causing
a lot of anxiety? It's the waiting that is important
to you now?

John: I don't know when it's got to happen. It's got to
happen pretty soon. I mean, I been out of the army
five years. It never bothered me too much when I
first got out. I thought about it; actually, I tried to
push it to the back of my mind. I didn't want to
think about it. I just left it go.

Pastor: The thought was rather painful then.

John: Yeah—well I didn't think about it. I blocked it out
completely.

Pastor: You were hoping with time it would go away; but
instead it began to grow larger, it began to be important in your life to see why this is?

John: Yeah.

Pastor: As time went on it didn't go away?

John: It got worse. I think what probably brought it back
to a head was that last week I was pallbearer at a
funeral. Almost couldn't carry the man; too much.
All I kept thinking of was that patrol over in Korea.
Kept going back, back. I just don't know what to
do. I know, even at home it's affecting things. The
other day, my wife and I got talking. Nothing too
bad. And I—I got nervous and hit her. I shouldn't

> do that; but it was like, I don't know. I just sort of lost control.

Pastor: All of a sudden something exploded that you couldn't control?

John: Yeah, I guess. Just out of nowhere. Wasn't her fault. I still don't know what to do. Why does he keep prolonging this thing? Get it over with. I just keep waiting, waiting.

Pastor: Waiting?

John: I don't know. I don't know! Even the kids notice it. I heard—the little boy, now five, born while I was in the army. My wife was about six months gone when I left, and then he came; and I got home to see him right before I left for Korea. And I heard him telling his mother, "What's wrong with Daddy these days? Why is he so cross?" I just sort of tried to forget about it; but he's right, I am cross. This business. I don't know what to do about it.

Pastor: The thinking of punishment is even affecting your home life, the punishment of God?

John: Yeah, uh-huh. Afraid it does. I just don't know what to do.

Pastor: Just like waiting for something that doesn't come?

John: But it's going to come. I don't know when. But it will come.

This case enables us to see how proclamation occurs in the process of perceptual restructuring.

First, this approach would focus on John's perceptions of himself. The war has clearly had a major effect on his self-perception, with the night in which he killed the five men playing a particularly large role in shaping his current perception of himself. That night he killed five men in a very systematic and deliberate way. Thus, he perceives himself as a cold-blooded murderer. Another aspect of that night's activities that may bear on his current self-perception was his separation from the other men on the patrol. As he puts it, "We got there and took care of our mission and on the way back it happened—we were ambushed. I sort of got cut off from the others." We cannot tell whether his getting "cut off" means that he deserted the other men, and therefore perceives himself as a coward. What we do know is that the others were shot at while he escaped. Thus, he seems to perceive himself as a person who did not deserve to survive.

The overall effect of the war on John's self-perception, then, was negative. However, he was apparently able to repress this change in self-perception until recently, when two critical events in his life brought this change home to him. The first was his pallbearer role at a funeral: "Almost couldn't carry the man; too much. All I kept thinking of was that patrol over in Korea." The funeral caused him to think of the men he had killed; it may also have caused him to think of the other men on his patrol. The second critical event was when he and his wife "got talking" and he "got nervous and hit her." This event brought home to him that he is capable of violent acts. Thus, he is coming to the awareness that he has aggressive, even destructive impulses that he is not able to control. But he has not yet assimilated this awareness into a new self-perception. It remains a foreign element in his self-understanding.

Second, this indirect approach to pastoral counseling would focus on John's perception of God. He views God as a kind of enemy soldier who is engaging in cruel and inhuman psychological warfare against him. God is stalking him even as he stalked the five men he killed that night, but God wants to torment him even further by withholding the inevitable punishment. In relating how his parents' punishment was swift and sure, John seems to long for the God of his childhood. But this view of God, however attractive, could not possibly survive his war experience. Images of God as parent are being replaced with images of God as the stalking enemy, and this latter image inhibits progress toward a new self-perception. This transformation in self-perception will depend, in part, on his gaining a new perception of God. John needs help in gaining new insights into how God deals with individuals who have carried a great burden of guilt for many years. These new insights would not be achieved merely by assuring John that he has suffered enough, that the psychological burden he has carried for five years has been worse than any further punishment that God could mete out to him. While such assurances may be factually true, they do little to help John acquire a new perception of God. Such a perception would probably draw on some facet of Christian affirmation that we can never adequately atone for our sins, even should this atonement take the form of serious, debilitating illness. And it would likely be in line with the Christian affirmation that God does not permanently harden his heart toward his own. If God stalks his prey, he also opens his heart to those who have suffered deeply and have come to him for solace. John asks, "Reverend, can God forgive people?" The ultimate answer to this question is neither the counselor's rather weak, "I think he can, what do you think?" (nondirective) or "Of course he can—that's his business!" (directive). Rather, the answer is another query such as, "Would God be God if he did not forgive?" (indirective).

Counseling in this case would be proclamatory, but in an indirective way. It would deal with John's negative self-perception by exploring his perception of God. While such an exploration might seem hopelessly abstract, as though the counseling session might turn into a theological debate, John will not realize a new self-image until he can "see" God in a new way—not only as enemy but as one who understands how it feels to be deeply and irrevocably guilty. Here, the Christian affirmation that Christ took our sinfulness on himself would be the key to the restructuring of John's perceptions of God and self. This is the perceptual restructuring that occurs when we see, perhaps for the first time, that Christ's suffering is God's face turned toward us.

Epilogue

The Funeral Sermon as Paradigm

Pastors often observe that their funeral sermons are most akin to pastoral counseling. Funeral sermons usually reflect the pastor's concern to assess the emotional and spiritual needs of the persons who have gathered together for the service. They also reflect the pastor's effort to enter into these persons' experience with empathic understanding. Funeral sermons are similar to pastoral counseling in that they are specifically designed for the present occasion. Pastors who say that they preach the same funeral sermon without regard to the identity of the deceased and the circumstances surrounding the death are held in some contempt by their fellow ministers. In like manner, pastors who say they give the same advice in counseling sessions regardless of the identity and circumstances of the counselee are subject to the same severe criticism by fellow ministers. In both cases, there is no general formula that "works." Given these similarities between the funeral sermon and the counseling session, we can think of the funeral sermon as a paradigm of the integration of preaching and pastoral counseling. I am not suggesting that every sermon should deal with the same problem as the funeral sermon (death and bereavement), or that grief counseling is the most important form of pastoral counseling. My point is that the funeral sermon is a dramatic example of the integration of preaching and pastoral counseling methods.

In discussing the funeral sermon as a paradigm of this

integration, I will focus on one sermon in particular. This sermon, which I will present in its entirety, was preached by Friedrich Schleiermacher on the occasion of the untimely death of his nine-year-old son Nathanael.[53] Not only does Schleiermacher give appropriate attention to theological diagnosis, but this diagnosis is largely responsible for the integration of the preaching and counseling functions of the sermon. By attending to the task of theological diagnosis, he simultaneously proclaims the gospel and provides counsel to the bereaved.

The Consoling Effect of Theological Diagnosis

Schleiermacher's sermon addresses the problem of finding any meaning in Nathanael's death that might bring consolation to the bereaved. The first section of the sermon identifies this problem. Schleiermacher acknowledges that "this one blow, the first of its kind, has shaken my life to its roots." The second stage of the sermon explores why he finds it difficult to discern any meaning in this death that would bring some semblance of consolation. The major reason that consolation is so difficult to realize is that he knows it will no longer be possible for him to carry out his fatherly intentions toward his son. While he realized that he could not expect to complete his son's upbringing because of his own advanced age, he did anticipate continuing to offer his son "faithful fatherly advice and strong support." Now, with his son's death, he will not be able to relate to his son in terms of these shared intentions. As he expresses it, "This charge, important above all others for the remainder of my life, to which my heart clung full of love, is now ineradicably stricken through."

What consolation is there when our deepest and most heartfelt intentions toward another being are permanently cut off? In the third segment of the sermon, Schleiermacher engages in a theological diagnosis of the consolations available to persons of faith. He considers and rejects two types of consolations before settling on a third. Thus, the diagnosis

discriminates between religious consolations that are ineffec-
tive and one that brings a genuine sense of resignation and
peace. The first consolation, based on the view that death
preserved his son from future temptations, is rejected because
it makes a mockery of the deep intentions that he wanted to
continue to express toward his son. It fails to recognize the
good work that had taken effect in Nathanael and was
already evoking positive responses from him. To say that
Nathanael's death saved him from a potential loss of faith in
later life denigrates the strong positive intentions of his parents and of the Christian community toward his growth and
development. It also fails to take account of the fact that this
nine-year-old boy had already come to share the same love
of God that prompted these intentions. For Nathanael's parents to seek consolation in the thought that he was spared
from spiritual and moral temptations is to imply that their
love would have had no real, enduring effect.

The second consolation that Schleiermacher finds wanting
suggests that Nathanael remains a participant in the "everlasting community" of those who have gone on before and
those who yet remain behind. Thus, the deep intentions that
had already begun to take effect in the boy had secured his
place in this everlasting community; and, therefore, while it
is true that his parents would not be able to continue to care
for him in direct ways, they would nonetheless participate
together in this community. Schleiermacher says that this
consolation lacks power because the images with which this
everlasting community is typically represented "leave behind
a thousand unanswered questions." This consolation fails to
provide genuine solace to one who is "too greatly accustomed
to the rigors and cutting edges of thinking." This consolation
does not denigrate the love expressed toward Nathanael
while he was yet alive. In this sense, it is less offensive than
the first consolation. Still, it tends to obscure the fact that
Schleiermacher's intentions toward the boy were cruelly terminated. The living and dead may continue to participate
together in an everlasting community. But the *basis* of the

relationship between them has been radically changed; one does not know whether one can depend on popular representations of this changed relationship.

The consolation that provides genuine solace, therefore, will have to be one that faces the fact that the father's intentions for his son will not be fulfilled. For Schleiermacher, this consolation has its basis in the promises of God's faithfulness as contained in the Scriptures. These promises indicate that parents' intentions toward their children will not have been in vain, even though they have not been brought to fruition, because these intentions were always subordinate to God's. The promises of the Scriptures, especially the powerful prayer ("Father, I would that where I am, they also may be whom Thou hast given me"), enable him to say with confidence that the Lord "truly watched over and guided" Nathanael. Thus, while his own intentions for the child were terminated, these desires were always subordinate to, but part of, the intentions which the Lord himself was expressing toward the child, and which are even now being brought to fruition. Nathanael's life is now in God's hands. With this consolation, Schleiermacher finds that he can relinquish the boy and his own intentions for his son's life. Moreover, because God himself began and is continuing a good work in Nathanael, those who are left behind can live with positive memories of their relationships with him. The guidance that God provided Nathanael is recognized as a rich blessing enabling the survivors to reflect on their experiences with the boy without any bitterness.

In the final section of the sermon Schleiermacher underscores the importance he places on our intentions toward one another by encouraging his listeners to relate to one another in the spirit of true Christian love. Whatever the nature of their relationships, whether parent to child, child to parent, or teacher to child, their deepest shared intentions toward one another need to be based on love because God *is* love. Schleiermacher concludes the sermon by praying that he will know the "fatherly love" of God, and that the pain his family has shared will become "a new bond of still more intimate love." These prayers and admonitions grow directly out of the theological diagnosis of the third stage of the sermon, a diagnosis that recognized that the deepest intentions of shared human experience are representations of God's deepest intentions toward his children.

Clearly, Schleiermacher's sermon integrates preaching and counseling through theological diagnosis. The fact that Schleiermacher is preaching a funeral sermon, one that involves deep personal anguish, does not cause him to neglect his pastoral responsibility to engage in careful theological diagnosis. He does not plead (as pastoral counselors sometimes do) that the emotional depths of the occasion do not lend themselves to theological discriminations. If anything, the need for theological diagnosis is even more urgent. Thus, Schleiermacher's funeral sermon integrates preaching and counseling through theological diagnosis. As an act of preaching, it proclaims that God's intentions continue to prevail even in death. As an act of counseling, it uses this proclamation to help the living to relinquish their claim on the dead.

The following is Schleiermacher's sermon as he preached it, except that I have divided the sermon into its four stages.

Schleiermacher's Sermon at Nathanael's Grave

Stage 1: Identification of the Problem

My dear friends, come here to grieve with this stooped father at the grave of his beloved child. I know you are not come with the intention of seeing a reed shaken by the wind. But what you find is in truth only an old stalk, which yet does not break even from this gust of wind that has suddenly struck him from on high, out of the blue. Thus it is! For a happy household, cared for and spared by Heaven for twenty years, I have God to thank; for a much longer pursuit of my vocation, accompanied by undeserved blessings; for a great abundance of joys and sorrows, which, in my calling and as a sympathetic friend, I have lived through with others. Many a heavy cloud has passed over my life; yet what has come from without, faith has surmounted, and what from within, love has recompensed. But now, this one blow, the first of its kind, has shaken my life to its roots.

Stage 2: Reconstruction of the Problem

Ah, children are not only dear pledges entrusted to us from God, for whom we must give account; not only inexhaustible subjects of concern and duty, of love and prayer: they are also an immediate blessing upon the house; they give easily as much as they receive; they freshen and gladden the heart. Just such a blessing was this boy for our house. As the Redeemer said that the angels of the little ones see the face of his Father in Heaven, so with this child it appeared to us as if such an angel beamed out from his countenance the kindness of our God. When God gave him to me, my first prayer was that fatherly love would never mislead me to expect more of the boy than was right; and I believe the Lord has granted me this. I know very well that there are children far more outstanding in gifts of mind, in eager alertness, and upon whom far greater expectations concerning what they will accomplish in the world could be raised, and I would rejoice should there be many of them. When I gave him the name he bore, not only did I want thereby to greet him as a precious and welcome gift of God [The name Nathanael derives from the Hebrew, "gift of God"]. I wanted at the same time to express my earnest wish that he might become like his Biblical namesake, a soul in which there is no falsehood; and this too the Lord has granted me. Honest and frank as our boy was, he looked everyone in the eye full of trust, doing only good to all, and we have never found anything false in him. And for this reason, my dear children whom I see around me here—because he was truthful —he also remained free from many sorrows which otherwise come even upon those of your age. A selfish nature was also something far from him, and he bore love and goodwill for all humanity. So he lived among us as the joy of the whole house. And when the time was come that it seemed necessary to transplant him to a larger community of young people and a wider circle of education, there too he began to acclimate himself and to thrive, and even the deserved and well-meant reprimands of his teachers fell on good soil.

Thus I had thought to follow him with fatherly eye still further, and I quietly waited to see to what degree his intellectual powers would further develop and to which area of human activity his inclination would turn. If I often said to myself—though in a sense wholly other than that which has now come to pass —that it would not be granted me to complete his upbringing [Schleiermacher was fifty-one years old when Nathanael was born], I was none the less of good courage. I regarded it as one more beautiful blessing of my calling that, in days to come, he would never fail to find faithful fatherly advice and strong support on my account, though I hoped he would not fail to find it on his own account as well.

This charge, important above all others for the remainder of my life, to which my heart clung full of love, is now ineradicably stricken through; the friendly, refreshing picture of life is suddenly destroyed; and all the hopes which rested upon him lie here and shall be buried with this coffin! What should I say?

Stage 3: Diagnostic Interpretation

There is one consolation, with which many faithful Christians soothe themselves in such a case, which already many beloved, friendly voices here have spoken to me in these days, and which is not to be simply dismissed, for it grows out of a correct assessment of human weakness. Namely, it is the consolation that children who are taken away young are in fact delivered from all of the dangers and temptations of this life and are early rescued into the sure Haven. And this boy would certainly not have been spared these dangers. But, in fact, this consolation does not want to take with me, I being the way I am. Regarding this world as I always do, as a world which is glorified through the life of the Redeemer and hallowed through the efficacy of his Spirit to an unending development of all that is good and Godly; wishing, as I always have, to be nothing but a servant of this divine Word in a joyful spirit and sense: why then should I not have believed that the blessings of the Christian community would be confirmed in my child as well, and that through Christian upbringing, an imperishable seed would have been planted in him? Why should I not have hoped in the merciful preservation of God for him also, even if he stumbled? Why should I not have trusted securely that nothing would be able to tear him out of the hand of the Lord and Savior to whom he was dedicated, and whom he had already begun to love with his childlike heart —for one of his last rational responses in the days of his sickness was a warm affirmation to the question of his mother, whether he loved his Savior rightly. And this love, even if it was not fully developed, even if it had undergone fluctuations in him: why should I not indeed have believed that it would never be extinguished for him, that it someday would have possessed him wholly? And as I would have had the courage to live through all this with him—to admonish him, to comfort, to lead—therefore this way of thinking is not as consoling to me as it is to many others.

Still others who grieve generate their consolation in another way, out of an abundance of attractive images in which they represent the everlasting community of those who have gone on before and those who as yet remain behind; and the more these images fill the soul, the more all the pains connected with death are stilled. But for the man who is too greatly accustomed to the rigors and cutting edges of thinking, these images leave behind a thousand unanswered questions and thereby lose much, much of their consoling power.

Thus I stand here, then, with my comfort and my hope alone in the Word of Scripture, modest and yet so rich, "It doth not yet appear what we shall be; but when it shall appear, we shall see Him as He is," and in the powerful prayer of the Lord, "Father, I would that where I am, they also may be whom Thou hast given me." Supported by these strong beliefs, then, and borne along by a childlike submission, I say from my heart, the Lord has given him: the name of the Lord be praised, that He gave him to me; that He granted to this child a life, which, even though short, was yet glad and bright and warmed by the loving breath of his Grace; that He has so truly watched over and guided him that now with his cherished remembrance nothing bitter is mixed. On the contrary, we must acknowledge that we have been richly blessed through this beloved child. The Lord has taken him: His name be praised, that although He has taken him, yet He has left us, and that this child remains with us here also in inextinguishable memories, a dear and imperishable individual.

Stage 4: Pastoral Intervention

Ah, I cannot part from the remains of this dear little form, ordained for decay, without now, after I have praised the Lord, expressing the most moving thanks of my heart: before all, to the dear half of my life through whom God gave me the gift of this child, for all the motherly love and trust which she bestowed on him from his first breath to his last, expired in her faithful arms; and to all my beloved older children, for the love with which they were devoted to this youngest and which made it easier for him to go his way, bright and happy, in the straight path of order and obedience; and to all the beloved friends who have rejoiced in him with us, and with us have cared for him; but especially to you, dear teachers, who made it your pleasure to take an active part in the development of his soul: and to you, dear playmates and schoolmates, who were devoted to him in childlike friendship, to whom he was indebted for so many of his happier hours, and who also mourn for him, since you would have liked to go forward with him still farther on the common way. And to all of those who have made this hour of parting more beautiful and celebrative for me, my thanks.

But with thanks it is always good that some gift be joined in return; and so, all of you, accept as a remembrance of this moment, so painfully significant for me, a well-meant gift of Christian admonition. My wife and I have both loved this child tenderly and with all our hearts, and what is more, amiability and gentleness are the ruling tone of our household. And yet, here and there, there steals through our memories of our life with this beloved child a soft tone of reproach. And so I believe that perhaps no one passes on, concerning whom those who lived most closely with him are completely satisfied when they examine themselves before God—even if the allotment of life has been as short as this one. Therefore let us all truly love one another as persons who could soon—alas, how soon!—be snatched away. I say this to you children; and you may believe me that this advice, if you follow it, will tarnish no innocent joys for you; rather it will surely protect you from many errors, even though they may be small. I say this to you parents; for even if you do not share my experience, you will enjoy even more unspoiled the fruits of this word. I say it with my sincerest thanks to you teachers; for even if you have to do with young people in numbers too great to allow you to develop a special relation with each individual, yet all the more must those things which you do to keep order and good discipline be infused with the right spirit of holy Christian love. Ah yes, let us all love one another as persons who could soon be separated.

Now, thou God who art love, let me not only resign myself to thy omnipotence, not only submit to thy impenetrable wisdom, but also know thy fatherly love! Make even this grievous trial a new blessing for me in my vocation! For me and all of mine let this communal pain become wherever possible a new bond of still more intimate love, and let it issue in a new apprehension of thy Spirit in all my household! Grant that even this grave hour may become a blessing for all who are gathered here. Let us all more and more mature to that wisdom which, looking beyond the void, sees and loves only the eternal in all things earthly and perishable, and in all thy decrees finds thy peace as well, and eternal life, to which through faith we are delivered out of death. Amen.

Notes

1. Edgar N. Jackson, *A Psychology for Preaching* (Channel Press, 1961), p. 141.

2. Edmund Holt Linn, *Preaching as Counseling: The Unique Method of Harry Emerson Fosdick* (Judson Press, 1966). Quotations from Linn and Fosdick in the following discussion are from this book.

3. Paul C. Vitz, *Psychology as Religion: The Cult of Self-Worship* (Wm. B. Eerdmans Publishing Co., 1977), pp. 69–72.

4. David K. Switzer, *Pastor, Preacher, Person: Developing a Pastoral Ministry in Depth* (Abingdon Press, 1979), Ch. 4.

5. Thomas C. Oden, *Kerygma and Counseling* (Westminster Press, 1966). Quotations by Oden in the following discussion are from this book. I am aware that Oden has been engaged recently in modifying some of his earlier positions on pastoral counseling, See Gaylord B. Noyce, "Has Ministry's Nerve Been Cut by the Pastoral Counseling Movement?" *The Christian Century,* Feb. 1–8, 1978, pp. 103–114. But the views I will be critiquing here are essentially unchanged. See his article "Recovering Lost Identity," *Journal of Pastoral Care*, Vol. 34, No. 1 (1980), pp. 4–19.

6. Wayne E. Oates, *Pastoral Counseling* (Westminster Press, 1974), p. 13. John B. Cobb, Jr., also supports this position in *Theology and Pastoral Care* (Fortress Press, 1977), p. 43.

7. Paul W. Pruyser, *The Minister as Diagnostician* (Westminster Press, 1976).

8. Cobb, *Theology and Pastoral Care,* pp. 58–62.

9. Wayne E. Oates has a brief but useful discussion of this issue in *Pastoral Counseling,* pp. 14–16. See also Daniel Day Williams,

The Minister and the Care of Souls (Harper & Row, 1977), pp. 46–51.

10. Henri J. M. Nouwen, *Creative Ministry* (Doubleday & Co., 1971). Quotations from Nouwen in the following discussion are from this book.

11. Thomas C. Oden, *The Structure of Awareness* (Abingdon Press, 1969), pp. 23–24.

12. Charles S. Gardner, *Psychology and Preaching* (Macmillan Co., 1918).

13. Jackson, *A Psychology for Preaching.* Quotations from Jackson in the following discussion are from this book.

14. Linn, *Preaching as Counseling,* p. 23.

15. James E. Dittes, *Minister on the Spot* (Pilgrim Press, 1970). Quotations from Dittes in the following discussion are from this book.

16. I have discussed these four elements of the counseling session at greater length in my book *Pastoral Care: A Thematic Approach* (Westminster Press, 1979), Ch. 3.

17. Rev. John Wesley, A.M., *Sermons on Several Occasions* (London: Epworth Press, 1944), pp. 360–370.

18. Martin Luther King, Jr., *Strength to Love* (Harper & Row, 1963), pp. 8–15.

19. W. D. White (ed.), *The Preaching of John Henry Newman* (Fortress Press, 1969), pp. 95–105.

20. Austin Farrer, *The End of Man* (London: SPCK, 1973), pp. 90–93.

21. Paul Tillich, *The New Being* (Charles Scribner's Sons, 1955), pp. 75–78.

22. Farrer, *The End of Man,* pp. 168–172.

23. Nouwen, *Creative Ministry,* p. xxi.

24. Oden, *Kerygma and Counseling,* p. 36.

25. Ibid., p. 27.

26. Ibid., p. 36.

27. Karl Barth, *Deliverance to the Captives* (Harper & Brothers, 1961).

28. Carl R. Rogers, *Client-Centered Therapy* (Houghton Mifflin Co., 1965), Ch. 2.

29. Ibid., Ch. 5.

30. Carl R. Rogers, *On Becoming a Person* (Houghton Mifflin Co., 1961), Ch. 5.

31. Ibid., Ch. 6.

32. Pruyser, *The Minister as Diagnostician,* Ch. 3.

33. William James, *The Varieties of Religious Experience* (New American Library of World Literature, 1958).

34. Newman S. Cryer and John M. Vayhinger (eds.), *Casebook in Pastoral Counseling* (Abingdon Press, 1962).

35. W. D. White (ed.), *The Preaching of John Henry Newman* (Fortress Press, 1969). The sermons discussed in the following section are all included in this edition of Newman's sermons.

36. Rev. John Wesley, A.M., *Sermons on Several Occasions* (London: The Epworth Press, 1944). The sermons discussed in the following section are all included in this edition of Wesley's sermons.

37. Paul Tillich, *The Shaking of the Foundations* (Charles Scribner's Sons, 1948). The sermons discussed in the following section are from this volume of Tillich's sermons.

38. William Scarlett (ed.), *Phillips Brooks: Selected Sermons* (E. P. Dutton, 1949). The sermons discussed in the following section are all included in this collection of Brooks's sermons.

39. Farrer, *The End of Man.* The sermons discussed in the following section are from this volume of Farrer's sermons.

40. Mary F. Wilson (tr.), *Selected Sermons of Schleiermacher* (London: Hodder & Stoughton, 1890). The sermons discussed in the following section are from this collection of Schleiermacher's sermons.

41. Wayne E. Oates, *Pastoral Care and Counseling in Grief and Separation* (Fortress Press, 1976), pp. 24–33.

42. Rogers, *Client-Centered Therapy,* pp. 52–56.

43. On this point, see Cobb, *Theology and Pastoral Care,* pp. 43ff.

44. John Henry Newman, B.D., *The Parting of Friends* (Newman Press, 1961), pp. 23–24.

45. The following discussion is an expansion of my article, "Biblical Models in Pastoral Counseling," *Pastoral Psychology,* Vol. 28, No. 4 (1979), pp. 252–264.

46. Seward Hiltner, *Pastoral Counseling* (Abingdon-Cokesbury Press, 1949).

47. Ibid., pp. 202–209.

48. Carroll Wise, *Psychiatry and the Bible* (Harper & Brothers, 1956), pp. 11ff.

49. Jay E. Adams, *Competent to Counsel* (Baker Book House, 1977), pp. 97–100.

50. James E. Dittes, *The Church in the Way* (Charles Scribner's Sons, 1967), *Minister on the Spot* (Pilgrim Press, 1970), *When the People Say No: Conflict and the Call to Ministry* (Harper & Row, 1979).

51. This sketch of the basic features of the parable is based on the following sources: Robert W. Funk, *Language, Hermeneutic, and Word of God* (Harper & Row, 1966), Ch. 5; John Dominic Crossan, *In Parables: The Challenge of the Historical Jesus* (Harper & Row, 1973); Sallie McFague TeSelle, *Speaking in Parables* (Fortress Press, 1975).

52. Nouwen, *Creative Ministry,* pp. 43–45.

53. Albert L. Blackwell, "Schleiermacher's Sermon at Nathanael's Grave," *Journal of Religion,* Vol. 57 (1977), pp. 64–75. Republished in *Pastoral Psychology,* Vol. 26, No. 1 (1977), pp. 23–36.